Hidden Nature

Also by Alys Fowler

The Thrifty Gardener
Garden Anywhere
The Edible Garden
The Thrifty Forager
Abundance

Alys Fowler is an award-winning journalist and passionate gardener. She started gardening in her early teens and later trained at the Royal Horticultural Society, the New York Botanical Garden and the Royal Botanic Gardens at Kew. She is the author of several books and writes a weekly column on gardening for *Guardian* Weekend magazine. She lives in Birmingham.

ALYS FOWLER

Hidden Nature

A Voyage of Discovery

HODDER

First published in Great Britain in 2017 by Hodder & Stoughton
An Hachette UK company

2

A CIP catalogue record for this title is available from the British Library

ISBN 9781473623026
eBook ISBN 9781473623033

Typeset in Sabon MT by Palimpsest Book Production Ltd, Falkirk, Stirlingshire

Printed and bound in Great Britain by Clays Ltd, St Ives plc

Hodder & Stoughton policy is to use papers that are natural, renewable
and recyclable products and made from wood grown in sustainable forests.
The logging and manufacturing processes are expected to conform
to the environmental regulations of the country of origin.

Hodder & Stoughton Ltd
Carmelite House
50 Victoria Embankment
London EC4Y 0DZ

www.hodder.co.uk

For my dearest Charlotte,
for without you there is none of this.

Introduction

My childhood dream was that I would grow up to be an adventurer. I knew it might be hard so I practised. I learnt to climb rock faces, to abseil into caves, to swim long distances in cold water, to sail small boats and surf makeshift rafts. I cycled everywhere on a 1920s sit-up-and-beg bike with no gears. When I was in my twenties a bike enthusiast told me it was an early example of a female racing model with narrow handlebars. I raced that bike into the ground.

I knew where you could swim in amber-coloured pools with speckled trout, and which trees to climb to find an owl's haunt. I trespassed in woods where I found deer traps that could have taken off my legs. I regularly tied a handkerchief to a stick and marched off to places I thought were far away. My childhood was solitary, but not lonely. I had a loyal dog and a host of imaginary friends. To the outside world, I'm quite sure I was a strange child, wandering through fields trailed by my dog, talking to myself, but I was perfectly content. I endured the company of other humans, particularly children, largely for adult approval.

I trained myself to walk far and fast. In my teens I could outstrip any long-legged male counterpart and delighted in doing so. I always carried a penknife and a bit of string – I still do. With my bike and a train timetable, I thought I could and would go everywhere. Secretly I wanted to be Gertrude Bell, the red-headed explorer and diplomat who mapped Jordan and Iraq, and went where many men had failed or feared to go. That she was a redhead in the desert made her especially appealing to me – even sunburn didn't get in her way.

Eventually I grew up and got married. I stopped climbing. I still biked but mostly out of necessity: to get to work across town. I still swam in cold water but in an urban park.

I'd fallen for a penniless artist. I don't think he'd mind me calling him that. He expanded everything about my world culturally, introduced me to artists, writers, musicians and movements, whole new ways of looking at the world. I loved that. I had also, as my master's degree in science, society and the environment had taught me, taken on the nature/culture dichotomy: the big divide, the perceived tension between nature, wild, untamed, and culture, filled with knowledge, belief, customs and art. I was living with it. Every day I cycled to work to write about one in terms of the other. In my early married life I wrote for a trade magazine about horticulture, largely about parks, bedding plants and, I seem to remember, waterproof jackets. Then I came home and consumed art, all the time longing to be outside, somewhere wild and vast and full of life.

We lived in a top-floor flat in east London. I kept pot plants perched precariously outside the window, and spent my after-work hours maintaining other people's gardens, always dreaming of a garden I could call my own.

We were living with another layer of the nature/culture divide: H has cystic fibrosis, a chronic illness. It's a long-term, life-threatening weakening of the lungs caused by a faulty gene. We were penniless then because he was an artist while I was an inexperienced young writer. In the eyes of the world, I was his carer. Of course, as we were young and in love, it did not feel like that. To me, we were brave and brilliant because we understood fragility. We lived for our moment. I didn't care who understood why I'd married so young and so quickly. I remember thinking that I had to worry about this moment, now, and that was all that mattered.

In retrospect, perhaps, I was a little fatalistic, though I would have argued long into the night that that wasn't where my philosophy lay. I was in love, I was young, and our future was not endless. We both knew that. My future, though, was a great expanse, like the wild space I longed to be in.

On my writer's wage, I worked around the clock to make ends meet and never quite managed it. Eventually I applied for a job in Birmingham and, for the first time ever, I had an inkling that I'd done well in the interview. As I wandered back to the station through bland shopping centres, I cried because I knew already that I would be leaving the capital I had grown to love. But Birmingham was cheap and I was tired.

*   *   *

I thought I'd do six months. It turned into a year, and I got my first garden. It was rented, had an overgrown lawn, neglected flowerbeds and a weed-ridden vegetable plot, but I thought it was heaven – even if it did have a huge leylandii growing in the middle. I missed London, but I had soil to call my own.

Nine years later, Birmingham is no longer a financial foot on the ladder: it's home. I own soil – my glorious sunny back garden, with a magnolia to welcome spring and two apple trees that are heavy with fruit by autumn. Birmingham gave us a spare room to turn into a studio, a kiln down the road and an allotment in the park. It gave us space, not acres, not wilderness, nothing fancy or out of the ordinary, just average space, dull perhaps, as Philip Larkin wrote:

> If that is what a skilled,
> Vigilant, flexible,
> Unemphasised, enthralled
> Catching of happiness is called.

*   *   *

And that is what I caught in Birmingham, a very ordinary kind of happiness. I think we both did.

Although I have tried – I have retraced my steps, searched across the foreign place that is my past, run across the map over and over again – I cannot pinpoint the moment when I knew, somewhere deep inside me, that I needed to be alone. Or, at least, that was what I thought. Now I see that it was not so much about being alone, though solitude was a necessary step, but that I needed to be somewhere unfamiliar: I needed a landscape that I didn't know by heart, that wasn't part of my heart. I needed to examine and re-examine somewhere that would fascinate and teach me. I needed somewhere in which I could absorb myself and, I hoped, soak up some of the unsettledness in me. Now and then something caught me off balance and I'd yearn for nature bigger than I could tend.

I thought of running away – I dreamt up plans to explore the far reaches of Bolivia and the mountains of central Asia. I had subscribed to adventure-travel magazines and dreamt of owning a tiny house somewhere wild. I'm very good at daydreaming. I'd say it's my strongest skill.

When I complained that life was keeping me city-bound, a friend suggested that I tackle the city as I might the wilderness. 'Climb the tallest building and spend the night under the stars on its summit, circumnavigate the city limits by cycle, canoe the canals,' he said.

The latter stuck. I did a little research. You needed a canoeing licence to cover you for indemnity and that was it. Anyone, it turned out, could float about on the canals. I asked around about boats. My friend Dave lives on a narrowboat in town and owned an inflatable canoe for such adventures. I persuaded him we should take it out for a paddle. We made a date.

Even though Dave is a seasoned narrowboater and has taken *Beau*, his boat, far and wide on the canal network, we were hesitant about being in an inflatable. I think we were worried that we would hit some unseen bit of metal and sink. Dave

4

decided to wear a wetsuit and I donned full waterproofs and wellies.

A wetsuit is not a great thing to go paddling a canoe in, unless you intend to get wet. You get very hot very quickly and it's a bit restrictive for arm action. I sat behind Dave and laughed as he turned beetroot with the effort. We didn't get far, but we did get to visit a side pool and look at waterlilies, and a dead end that was too silted up for any heavy boat so I got to explore a little canal ecology.

As it turned out, Dave was wise to wear a wetsuit, not because we hit any underwater hazards but because his inflatable canoe has a plug in the bottom. It is well hidden below folds of plastic, and unless you're aware of it the boat slowly fills with water. As we were both waterproofed, it was fairly late in the expedition when we noticed that we were no longer floating on the water but rather lowering into it. We managed to get to the side before we began to sink. I remember lying on the towpath in a fit of giggles that we'd made such a rookie error, and that Dave's wetsuit had been the right choice for the wrong reason.

That trip whetted my appetite and I started to look into boats that would pack down or fold. But all the canoes I saw were too heavy for me to carry alone. Still, the idea that there was somewhere on my doorstep for me to explore was appealing. Even more so because that space had been largely ignored. Long-standing citizens of Birmingham, those born and bred in the city, never to leave, hadn't contemplated paddling the canals. Access seemed to be left largely to the dedicated, if mildly eccentric, narrowboating community. If in other cities narrowboats offer cheap accommodation, in Birmingham things are different: there's plenty of cheap accommodation in the city. Birmingham narrowboaters are true enthusiasts, either committed to a life with a movable home or restoration addicts with beautiful old working boats, polished and painted to perfection.

I continued to quiz Dave about the Birmingham Canal Network. He is a man with a great brain that needs constant exercise and, luckily for me, has a degree in ecology, plus a nerdy love of his favourite hobby. He told me of places thick with waterlilies and the flowering rush, *Butomus umbellatus*, of large pikes and eels, of disused waterways, hidden tracks and ghost canals, filled in under shopping malls and housing developments. Now that he's a planning officer for the council, he's taken his love to all the canal-side buildings, and told me of wonderful crumbling façades and grade-one-listed factories. Outside a bar one evening, I asked him if he thought paddling the network was achievable: I figured I had till early autumn before the water grew too cold and all the green things disappeared.

He sent me a quaint online map that makes the canals look rather small until you realise that much of the Birmingham Canal Network isn't in Birmingham but reaches out to Wolverhampton, Dudley and beyond. It was not so much that I didn't want to go to Wolverhampton or Dudley, but that I knew those outer reaches were going to be challenging in terms of getting there and back in the time I had allotted for my adventures. I was not taking time off to paddle. It had to fit around my life – an afternoon, a couple of hours over lunch, an early-evening paddle, with longer trips at weekends. I was seeing the paddle as the commute to my writing life. I wasn't prepared to admit it then, but paddling was going to compete with gardening. I couldn't admit either that I wasn't just prepared to allow it to happen: a bit of me was excited by the thought of walking away from the garden.

Using the city limits as my furthest reach, I drew a line around a map of Birmingham. Any canal that fell inside this, I would paddle. Dave and I made tentative plans for further expeditions.

1

I stuffed my wellingtons, rubber gloves, plastic bags and a large chocolate éclair into a bag. I put on two jumpers, two coats, and grabbed the car keys. Driving at night in Birmingham is a magical experience. It is a car city, a post-war metropolis with motorways snaking through and around, under and over it. On paper it must have been a town planner's dream, all those grey rivers of tarmac washing people through a gleaming new world of shiny skyscrapers. The reality is, as everyone knows, not quite as sparkling, but while it's still early enough for the city to be blanketed by darkness, you get a little glimpse of that dream.

You can drive fast. The city lights twinkle as you rise above and dip below the inhabitants. Birmingham roundabouts are dull by day, but at night you learn of the town planner's delight, a curve in the roads, a vista big enough to let you put your foot down and claim the city. Like all town-planning failures, Birmingham roads are flawless till you put other users on them. I wound my way across my city to the sound of the shipping forecast, enjoying the inky darkness and how pretty the city looked.

The first blast of cold air jolted me – my warm bed, then a warm car, so I was unprepared. I zipped up everything and put on the rubber gloves in the faint hope they would make a difference. I waited at the bottom of the bridge. Everything was still on the canal, the neon glow of the streetlights barely rippling on the water. Even the ducks were tucked up somewhere.

Dave and his girlfriend, Louise appeared across the top of the bridge and came down to meet me. Dave handed me a high-visibility jacket, and Louise agreed to keep a look-out while we went down.

The day before, I'd met Dave on his boat to go and see the drained canal. He was giddy with excitement at having found someone who actually wanted to discuss the muddy bottom. 'I'm going in. My curiosity has got the better of me. Six a.m. tomorrow morning, I think it will just be getting light enough, but there shouldn't be anyone around. I am going to wear a high-vis jacket so people think I'm official.'

Before he could go any further, before I'd even seen the drained canal, I'd signed up.

Dave and I had met years before, working at the BBC. That first afternoon I ordered him to come on an afternoon swimming jaunt in the River Stour with my team and not to tell our boss what we were up to – we were supposed to be prepping for a shoot. He gamely took up the challenge of swimming with strangers and never said a word to anyone. It cemented our friendship. He'd often drive me early in the morning to the garden where we filmed *Gardeners World*, music blaring to a play list he'd created the night before to amuse me. There was a track to get us going, another based on reggae, one for cold damp mornings, and something for when TV was bringing us down.

Not long after I met Dave he bought a narrowboat and I owe him greatly for introducing me to the canals of Birmingham and their history. Any excuse to go on a jaunt with his boat, he'd fill it with people and head out. He's one of the brightest people I know. He has a strange and wonderful brain that loves gathering detail, so in many ways the canal, with its rich history, is a perfect world for him to explore.

The canal network is more than two hundred years old, and an opportunity to see the lining of its belly is rare. I doubt it will happen again in my lifetime. So, if there was a chance to stand in the heavy pollution of Victorian silt, I'd take it.

The Worcester Bar Basin at Gas Street is one of the oldest parts of the canal. It sits in the heart of town, a stone's throw from the Symphony Hall. If you have to live in town, there is no better location. The basin's history is steeped in industrial politics. Stand one side of the Bar and you're on the Worcester and Birmingham Canal. Stand the other, and you're on the Birmingham Canal Network. A thin island, seven feet of Victorian bricks, meant that for years the canals didn't actually meet. Boatmen would have to unload to the towpath from one boat to another by hand. The most precious resource was ownership of the water, and the Birmingham Canal Network was not sharing it with Worcester. In 1815 they finally came to an agreement and built a stop lock through the Bar.

Today this stop-lock looks like one of many baffling locks that punctuate the canal. I've always assumed it was some engineering feat about moving water over land, not a solution to a few stubborn men arguing over money.

The Bar is in part why you can live in the centre of town on a boat. There have always been narrowboats here, many of them fine examples because the basin is a bit of a showcase for narrowboat enthusiasts. Walk under that narrow tunnel and you leave the clamour of Broad Street and step into a rarefied world of polished brass, coal-smoke fires, the clank of metal hulls and old men ready to tell you anything and everything you've ever cared to know about these waters. The basin is a hugely desirable place to moor, berths rarely come up, and I have a feeling that once you've mastered the impossible bidding system that secures you one, you may also have to pass an exam in canal history. The basin, as *The Birmingham Canal Navigations* booklet puts it, is a 'mecca for local waterways enthusiasts'.

Just up from the basin on the Worcester branch the canal had started to leak. This is not, I think, unusual. The canal's basin is porous as it is essentially puddled clay; the sides are bricks and mortar, which are forever leaking a little. However, this section sits above the railway. It was seeping into a disused tunnel, but eventually it would leak onto the main line that carries trains from Penzance to Inverness. Thus the canal was being drained to plug the leak. Initially it was decided to drain the whole basin, which would have meant moving out all the narrowboats, but at the last minute several old narrowboat boys taught the young engineers a thing or two about canals and how you dam them.

During all of this there was plenty of talk about diamond rings. The basin is a short cut to the bawdy strip and dancehalls of Broad Street, and everyone seemed to have at least one tale of engagement rings flung into the canal. So, I wasn't surprised that by now Dave had not only spent hours peering into the sludge of the drained canal but had identified several treasures he wanted. As we walked along the towpath, spying through the barrier, he named what he saw as rightfully his. He wanted the sunglasses, the goblet 'that might be the Holy Grail or just a beer glass', a Victorian scuttle, a console of some sort that he was mildly obsessed with, to the extent that 'I have to know what it's for', and some bunny plastic ears. Apart from a very large and handsome terracotta pot that must once have been on someone's balcony, it was hard to spot anything else in the mud that one might want. There were numerous beer and gin bottles and that seemed to be that. But it seemed important that I name at least one find if I was to come on the mission to climb down into the mud and reclaim the treasures.

I stared very hard . . . and then I saw them: mussel shells. 'I want the mussels,' I blurted out.

Dave turned first to the mud and then to me. 'You want the mussels?' he repeated, a little incredulous.

We decided that the mussels were too big to have come from one of the canal-side restaurants so they must be freshwater mussels. That was all the reason I needed to go down into the mud.

Mudlarking is an old practice. The name comes from the urchins who used to trawl the banks of the Thames for anything they could sell. It was a bottom-rung job for eighteenth- and nineteenth-century children and the elderly, but it came with a certain freedom: you made your own hours in accordance with the tides, and I guess there was always the glimmer in the mud of the next find that might bring you your fortune. Today most mudlarks have a metal detector but, for one morning, we'd join the ranks without, once we'd got round the barrier.

It took a little rearranging but soon we slipped down the towpath and chose a suitable spot to jump down into the canal. It is seven or eight feet deep, and at various times rubble has been poured into it to block suspected holes so there were small islands between the watery mud for us to jump onto.

Dave stepped gingerly into the mud. It looked firm enough and there were already some footprints in it, but that was a deception. It quickly became clear that the mud was like quicksand and far deeper than we had imagined. We were stuck, hopping from rubble island to rubble island. The beautiful terracotta pot would remain a buried treasure. So would the Victorian coal scuttle, which disintegrated in Dave's hand as he tried to pull it up. A pair of sunglasses, the bunny ears and a frying pan were all easy pickings, so I left him poking about to go and look at the shells. Torch in one hand, I bent down to pick up the first. The mud slurped as I pulled it free.

The stench of industrial silt was overpowering, rotting and metallic. The pearlescent inside of the shell gleamed, while the outside was covered with a thick black treacle of slime and mud. I put it into my plastic bag, then picked up another and another. At some point I collected a closed shell. The lips didn't entirely meet and there was a line of what looked like hair, which retracted inside. I felt the weight of the shell, turned it over and tried gently to prise it open. It resisted. 'These mussels,' I whispered, 'are alive . . . Dave!' I shouted. 'Some of these mussels are alive! They live here!'

Dave had collected a bunch more empty shells and one live mussel. He offered me the empty ones and said he'd keep the live one as a pet.

We'd explored as many islands of rubble as we could reach and it was time to get out. In the breaking of day, the dam looked precarious and thus ominous. As Dave climbed out I spotted something in the mud and my heart skipped a beat. It looked like a big fat finger. All the canals' darkest tales end in dead bodies, sunk in murky waters never to be found again. I steeled myself and peered down to look at it. I prodded it with one of the mussel shells and scraped at the mud. I exposed what looked like a knuckle, then dug a bit further. There was a small fisted hand. I'd found the right arm of a superhero's spacesuit. Relieved, I pulled it out and shoved it into my pocket.

I was too small to climb out of the canal so Dave hauled me out by my wrists. I felt I'd earned my mudlark stripes.

Back in the warmth of his boat we drank tea until the dawn chorus of a lone blackbird ended. As I left, Dave handed me two publications: a photocopied *Birmingham Canal Navigations*: *A Cruising and Walking Guide*, published in the 1980s, which detailed not only every inch of the canal network but the nearest fish and chips and Chinese eateries, all drawn by hand, and a pale-blue pamphlet called *The Other Sixty Miles – a survey of abandoned canals of Birmingham and the Black Country*. The reading list for my adventure.

* * *

When I got home I took out my treasures and placed them in a washing-up bowl to clean them. Dave, with his former environmental officer hat on, had made perfectly clear how polluted the canal was so I carefully washed the mussels with washing-up liquid, wearing rubber gloves, endlessly changing the water until it was no longer murky. In the clean tap water the mussels gleamed and their pearlescent insides glistened.

The outer rim of the mussels was inky black with papery growth rings; towards the centre they were a dirty, rusty brown. Some had a deep-green band. The mother-of-pearl inner iridescent layer is known as nacre and is made up of chalk that is secreted by the mantle in the mussel. Then there is another chalky layer, and an outer final layer, the periostracum, that is much like skin. It is this that makes up the papery growth rings on the outside of mussels. That final layer is important in protecting the mussel from acids as they would dissolve the chalk, thinning the shell.

On the outside there were two worn areas just by the dorsal side, the part where the mussel hinges together, that are pearly white and exposed. I studied the shell anatomy online and came to the conclusion that these must be the umbones or beaks, the oldest part of the shell. From here the growth lines ripple out, and I meticulously counted them. My mussels had been sitting down there since around the seventies.

Duck mussels are survivors in polluted places. They clean up as they go. Large freshwater mussels live in the muddy, silted layer of slow-running rivers, streams, lakes, ponds and canals. They live on plankton, filtering it through the water they breathe, their frilled lips sieving out waste material. They are a very important step in cleaning things up, filtering up to forty litres of water a day.

Duck mussels like standing water – they are not much into movement, though they like to wander and will quack their way around the floor, opening their shells to use their foot to drag themselves forward. It is slow, cumbersome work, but off they go. If you put a duck mussel in a clean, clear garden pond or a large aquarium you can watch it move around. I find this slightly unnerving, though I can't quite explain why I think it shouldn't move about.

One reason it moves is because standing bodies of water are actually very unstable compared to the sea. They dry out, and the water quality changes; they warm up, and the water quality changes; they flood, and the water quality changes. Nutrients, oxygen and pH can fluctuate seasonally, and anyone who's going to survive there can only do so with tenacity. A pond mussel can survive in a dried-out body of water for up to two months as long as it can dig itself into the mud to keep hydrated.

I cleaned the mussel shells very carefully to try to remove some of the pollution. When they are wet they are quite something to look at, but as they dry out they not only lose their pearlescent sheen, but start to pop and crack. I sat them in a pretty glass bowl on my desk, and for weeks heard intermittent cracks and pops as the shells started to show tiny fractures.

*   *   *

A freshwater pearl mussel can live for up to 150 years; my humble duck mussels were about the same age as me, thirty-seven. They are in the heart of the city, among beer glasses and lost engagement rings, and they are breeding. Every time I pass the spot I think of my mussels deep down in that dark murky land. I think of them growing old, filtering out.

2

I wrote to a nice man called Rob at Back Country Biking – he is the only person selling pack rafts in the UK – and asked him not to laugh at my idea of an adventure. I asked him this because his website is full of burly men whitewater-rafting down impossible rivers and biking across terrain that I didn't think I could push a bike over. My towpath, flat water and folding bike looked decidedly pedestrian in that light. He didn't laugh, and instead sent me a video of some earnest young skateboarder in Sweden taking a pack raft for 'some urban action'. And – this clinched the deal for me – he added, 'Don't forget you can get on a bus with both a pack raft and a Brompton [bike]!' Finally, he offered some advice about portage, when you carry a boat and its cargo between navigable waters: 'The canals up here will not allow you through the locks any more unless you are in a motor or sail boat. To be fair, a lock with the turbulence of the water coming in is not a nice place to be. I'd go for the portage any day.'

He advised on which size boat would take me, my day luggage and the bike, and which was the best paddle to 'take abuse', from which I inferred he meant I would probably wreck the paddle with my amateur moves.

I took a deep breath and pressed 'buy' on a thousand pounds' worth of blow-up plastic. Then I paced the house till it appeared.

A pack raft is a sort of adult blow-up dinghy, a miniature kayak if you like, that can pack down into a rucksack and thus be carried for part of the journey. The ingenuity lies in the fact that they are blown up not with a pump but with a silk bag roughly the size of a pillow. In this you trap air, twist, so the pillow is pumped up, then squeeze the air into the boat. The silk pillow weighs very little and packs down to the size of a satsuma. It's an ultra-light, super-efficient article, perhaps one of the joys of the boat design.

My boat, an Alapacka, started off as a whitewater-rafting craft for the back of beyond in Alaska. These vessels are for extreme adventures. They are not fast boats, they are not efficient boats, but they are boats that take you where others can't. They are tough, light and very quick to blow up. A pack raft can be trans-ported anywhere – to the remotest lake, the furthest beach, distant wild rivers or, in my case, the local canal, by human power alone. To secret places, where even other kayaks can't go, in low water because of its unique flat bottom. It is a burgeoning sport. Pack-rafters are adventurous types, remaking the rules for where you can get to and how.

The boats are expensive partly because they are hand made, often to order. I could have bought a dinghy or a cheaper, heavier boat, but I wanted independence above anything else. I wanted to be able to run out of the door when a spare hour or two became available. I had tried Dave's blow-up canoe but it was so heavy you needed to transport it by car and you had to use a pump to inflate it. And, more than anything else, I wanted to be alone. As Audrey Sutherland, the great female paddler and traveller, wrote in *Paddling North*, about kayaking on the south-east coast of Alaska, 'Go simple, go solo, go now.' That had been my mantra ever since I finished her book. I might not have been tackling the wilds of Alaska, but I had an inkling that there was a wilderness out there to explore, even if it was bound by my city limits.

The idea was that I could strap the boat to my back, get on my folding bike and cycle to the canal, blow up the boat, fold the bike, strap it onto the front and paddle as far as I could, then hop back on the bike and pedal home again. It's a simple, light, small set-up. The boat and I are about the same length. I liked everything about it.

I wanted an earthy-green version, but there was a wait for that colour. If I delayed, I knew I'd think twice about spending a thousand pounds on a boat – I might even chicken out – so I bought the bright-red one. My rationale was that at least the bike and the boat would match. I bought a red lifejacket from the children's section in a closing-down sports shop and felt suitably co-ordinated. Lately, when I've been the most conspicuous thing on the canal, I've often wished I'd held out for the green boat, and that colour-coordinating my adventure hadn't been quite such a girlish flourish.

* * *

The boat arrived at the weekend, neatly packed in a brown cardboard box. By this point I had watched endless YouTube videos about how to blow it up, using its silky blue bag. After a few failed attempts, I got the knack of trapping air and blew it up in my sitting room. I sat in my boat, and the dog looked warily at it, then tiptoed around it, quite sure it might do something unpredictable, like burst. This was a warning as to how all wildlife would treat a giant red inflatable, but just then, I was very pleased to sit in it on my sea of carpet and pretend to paddle.

H, my husband, came downstairs and was mildly unimpressed, telling me I would 'probably drown'. I pointed to my child's lifejacket – I wasn't entirely sure it would support my weight – and said, 'I'm hardly whitewater-rafting on a canal.' Then I packed the whole thing up, found a rucksack it would fit into and ran out of the house, gleefully shouting that I'd be down by the Mailbox – once a Royal Mail sorting office, now an exclusive shopping mall – and if he hadn't heard from me in several hours to call a lifeguard.

* * *

I took the bus to the Mailbox in the centre of Birmingham, grinning the whole way, fingering the blade of the paddle and imagining how triumphant I would look on this adventure. I chose the Mailbox because the number fifty bus would take me to it, and it's around the corner from the basin, where Dave moored his boat and there would be plenty of people about. If I did fall in, I reckoned someone would probably pull me out.

I called Dave to tell him I'd launch beside his boat, but he'd gone away for the weekend. He reminded me that I must pass all boats on the right and to check before I entered any tunnel that no boats were coming from the other direction: many canal tunnels are the width of single narrowboat.

By the time I got to the basin the weather had turned from sunny and blustery to a gale, but I decided this would make trapping air with the bag to inflate the boat much easier. That there were waves on the canal seemed to pass me by. Once the boat was half inflated I realised that keeping it in one place was going to be hard work as the wind tried to whip it away. I straddled it and continued to trap air. Once I'd decided it was inflated enough, I put together the folding paddle and donned my lifejacket. Getting into the boat from the edge is not complicated but I didn't do it elegantly. Some old boat boys looked on curiously, and one shouted, 'Are you sure you want to go paddling in this weather?' I waved my canoeing boat licence at them and pushed off.

Within seconds I had drenched myself with my poor paddle action. I also didn't seem to be getting anywhere fast. The boat waddled along, like a duck, and I had to lean hard on the paddle to move it anywhere in particular. I decided to go down to the National Indoor Arena and Sealife Centre (oh, the irony of those poor sea otters in landlocked Birmingham) that are located by the canal, which meant passing through my first tunnel, the Broad Street Tunnel. It was a lot harder work than I had imagined, but I checked that the tunnel was free and started to paddle.

Just as I reached the mouth I saw a narrowboat heading towards me and that everyone on the towpath was walking much faster than I was paddling. It occurred to me that the narrowboat was going to be on top of me before I could manage to get out of the tunnel. I panicked – various onlookers panicked on my behalf. I turned the boat too quickly and it spun back to its original position, a full 360 degrees, and I panicked some more. I paddled frantically and just made it out the way I'd come in before the narrowboat appeared. I paddled like mad to the side and clung on for dear life as the boat passed me. I tried to seem calm and composed but I just looked ridiculous – everyone around me confirmed this by staring at me as if I was mad.

Once the boat had passed, I decided that the National Indoor Arena was perhaps too far and that travelling with the wind would make more sense. I whipped down towards the Mailbox and felt a little more confident. That was until another narrowboat appeared. It was the Mailbox tour boat, filled with tourists, who waved at me and took lots of pictures. At this point I lost control and was spinning round and round as the canal whipped into peaks of white waves, the wind howled and I tried to wave back at the tourists – or, at least, to make my wave look like just that and not a cry for help. The tour boat, with little else to do on that now rather gloomy day, did a slow sweep around me so that the tourists could take more pictures, and I had to pretend that was why I was there, grinning with gritted teeth.

I longed to get back onto land. Once the tour boat had had its fun, I decided to get out by a dead-end canal that opened onto the back of the Mailbox. I sped along on the waves. The wind was now so strong that it was tipping the canal water up onto the towpath. I decided my best bet was to corner the boat in the dead end and attempt to crawl out in one piece. The boat spun onto the edge and I put the paddle on the towpath. The wind whipped it away, and I watched it trundle off down the path. A hundred and sixty pounds' worth of carbon fibre rattled away from me.

I was now paddleless and still stuck on the water. I found a hitching ring to cling to and dragged myself out when a wave flipped the boat. I landed on my back in a puddle with the boat on top of me. A Mailbox security guard peeled the boat off and peered at me, utterly confused. I sat up and tried to act as if that had been exactly how you should remove yourself from the canal. That part of the Mailbox was lined with bars, and I noticed that most windows were crammed with onlookers laughing at my exploits. I packed up the boat as quickly as I could, rescued my errant paddle and scurried away. Exhausted, I took myself to get some falafel as a commiseration prize for such an ungraceful launch.

When I finally got home, dripping wet, I found a small tag I had pulled out of the bottom of the boat. It bore the instructions for paddling:

Rule 1. Your boat is designed to spin so that it can bounce off obstructions.

Rule 2. Your boat is very buoyant: it will spin in high winds.

Rule 3. Your raft has multiple 'grab loops' onto which cords and mooring lines can be fastened.

I'd failed to read any of that and thus had spent an hour spinning around in a panic. I turned on the computer and spent the next few days watching endless YouTube videos on how to pack raft, how to paddle, how to capsize and right the boat, how to do an 'octopus' over shallow water, how to turn the boat into a shelter, how to blow the boat up mid-paddling and how to get in and out without looking like an idiot.

Several trips later, I'd learnt how to use all that spinning to my advantage. My paddling got smoother and I drenched myself less. I learnt how to secure the backpack and the bike so they didn't endanger my progress and to install towlines, grablines and waterproof bags so I could carry my phone, licence and notebook safely.

3

The day unfurled with spring. April was bright, blue and sweet-smelling. Everything stretched out in the new light, winter-weary muscles flexing to turn to the sun. I sat on the top floor of the number fifty to look at bus-stop roof gardens. Mostly there were thousands of sycamore seedlings, sprouting in the drainage channels, unaware that their brilliant beginning would soon strangle them with no root run.

There's something very pleasing about being on a bus with a paddle strapped to your rucksack – the idea that an adventure can start with something as prosaic as a daysaver ticket. I took the bus into the centre of town and walked back to the Gas Street Basin near the Mailbox. There, I blew up the boat with comparative ease. I was getting better at trapping the bag with pillowcase amounts of air. I'd learnt to be slow and methodical, although my heart was already racing at the thought of the journey. I secured my pack, made sure the waterproof bag for my phone was tied down and looped a rope from the boat to my arm to stop it floating away when I got out.

I'd learnt the wrong way that this was essential. I made a slip knot at the end of the rope and created a loop I could sling over my arm; it would allow me to unattach the boat from myself quickly, if necessary. Pack-rafting is a world where you want to hold onto everything for as long as possible until you can't. Then you need to ditch it quickly.

On the water, I noted with pleasure how quickly my paddling was improving. With no wind to compete against this time, I picked up speed and quickly made my way to Old Turn Junction where, in the middle of a canal, there is a roundabout with a signpost to various branches: the Main Line to Wolverhampton, to Soho, or the Birmingham and Fazeley Canal to Aston. I got a kick out of seeing my adventure signposted and headed off to Soho, waved on by a class of nine-year-olds eating their lunch on the steps of the Indoor Arena. In the coming weeks I learnt that Birmingham still firmly upholds the tradition of the gongoozler – a curious onlooker idly observing canal life going by.

The term 'gongoozler' is bargee slang. The canals had a working itinerant community, the bargees, who lived solely on the water and thought of themselves as distinctly different people from those who lived on the land. And with it they had their own terms and language to underline this separation. 'Gongoozler' is a lost word, like 'bridge 'ole', the channel under a bridge narrowed by the width of the towpath, or 'butty boat', derived from 'buddy' or 'mate', a non-powered boat towed by a motor boat, or 'joshers', boats once belonging to Fellows, Morton and Clayton Ltd, and named after Joshua, one of the owners. Lost words from a lost time, but a few, like 'bridge 'ole' and 'gongoozler' are well worth keeping hold of.

Gongoozlers love flights of locks – it's hard not to be thrilled by the opening of the paddles and the slow pushing of the heavy balance beams. They love hanging over bridges to peer below, nodding and waving. Sometimes they comment on the strange sight of a woman in a bright-red inflatable dinghy going nowhere particularly fast. Nearly everyone stops to say hello when you're paddling.

Later on, at the Soho loop, I had a leisurely conversation with two young people high on something or just blind drunk. They were dancing together as I approached and continued to dance apart and then together, him hugging her from behind and swaying in time to our conversation, both waving beer cans.

They wanted to know how much the boat had cost, and for a second I felt wary, but it was quickly apparent that they were way too high to do anything more than dance about our conversation. We talked about where I was heading and they waved me on.

The boat afforded great safety. Out in the middle no one could touch me, and that is a freedom that's hard to find in the darker corners of any city, particularly for a woman. The water was too dirty and the bottom too unknown for anyone to get to me. They could taunt or hurl, but I learnt how the boat and I could become one and move quickly when we needed to.

I left the couple slow-dancing into certain oblivion in the shade of Asylum Bridge, just past Winson Green Prison, with its own canal tunnel into its dark recesses. Despite the sunlight dancing on the water and the pussy willows bursting forth, this didn't feel like any sort of idyll. The water was strewn with rubbish and had a slick of green scum bubbling at the edges. The other towpath users were naturally wary of anyone they met. No one said hello there and the only joggers were male. The two women I saw were walking pit bulls and, when I said hello, refused to acknowledge my presence, even though I matched their pace and thus made for an odd shadow.

The wind whipped up on the final stretch of the loop, and the canal was now built up on either side with old brick factories. Although the bricks were drenched in sunlight and a peacock butterfly basked in the warmth, the water became choppy and that last stretch took all the energy left in my arms. By the time I reached the Main Line, I was glad to leave the Soho Loop behind and felt no need to return any time soon.

* * *

A few days later I decided to do Icknield Port Loop, which sits below Edgbaston Reservoir, once known as Rotton Park Reservoir and often comically misspelt as Rotten Park. It was once a tiny natural spring called Roach Pool and part of a huge 300-acre medieval deer park, though now it is hard to imagine such.

Canals need water, lots of it, and a small pool can become a large reservoir if necessary. In 1824, Thomas Telford enlarged the pool to supply water to the Birmingham Canal Network, via the loop. It was excavated to a depth of 13 yards and covers more than fifty-eight acres, making it the largest expanse of water in Birmingham. It looms rather eerily over the canal. Digging a giant pool out of a small one does not guarantee you all the water you will need and, like the rest of the network, the reservoirs are full of stolen water. Titford Reservoir, another natural pool widened in the late eighteenth century, feeds into Edgbaston Reservoir, as do several other side streams and small pools. The Industrial Revolution tamed Birmingham's streams, pools and springs and fed them ruthlessly into the canals.

At the beginning of the loop all I could see was birches, willows and the odd crumbling façade of the glassworks. This was what I'd come to find on the boat: lost wilderness in hidden parts of the city. Running along the edges of the canal, a ribbon of brilliant yellow was so searing that it seemed unnatural. Coltsfoot, *Tussilago farfara*, tiny, impoverished coltsfoot, was blooming everywhere. It was traditionally used for coughs and chest infections. '*Tussilago*' comes from the Latin *tussis*, meaning cough, and, *ago*, meaning to drive or pass. It seems apt that in a world where heavy industrial pollution must have shortened everyone's breath coltsfoot grew in such abundance.

Coltsfoot is a flower of disturbed ground; it likes impoverished edges, shingle, dunes, eroding cliffs, scree, riverbanks and wayside verges. The flowers appear before the leaves, giving them an other-worldly appeal. The stems arch upwards, blushed pink, and the flowers unfold their rays for any passing pollinators to land and sup, and finally, when the job is done, close their petals inwards to reveal their orange undersides. They were so bright that, for a moment, I wondered if they were a different species. I moored to take a look.

Up close, the bank on which they grew was full of broken glass from the factory. Like a pebble beach made from a rainbow of hues, it glittered and gleamed, enchanting, lethal. The weather had done little to smooth those shards and fragments of glass among the brick rubble, yet from that strange substrate bloomed not just coltsfoot but mushrooms and fairy-sized beds of moss.

As I peered into the miniature world, the boat started to rock and water lapped at the sides. I realised a little too late that a narrowboat was coming and almost lost my paddle. I'd thought I was alone in that wonderful wilderness, but here again came a tour boat. I felt plagued by tour boats.

Three old men sat inside, gazing out from the plastic windows. They looked lost or bored, and we eyeballed each other as they passed. I couldn't see the captain, who was hidden in a little purpose-built cabin, and wondered briefly if he was Charon, the ferryman of Hades, carrying the souls of newly deceased narrowboaters across the River Styx. I couldn't imagine who else might want to take those tours.

Round the bend, I entered the Oldbury Section Maintenance Yard, also known as the Boat Yard, it being the last one left around there. Built in 1845, it is a thing of wonder with beautiful, Gothic-arched windows on the superintendent's office, a canalside depot, wharfage and docking facilities. To this day, it works just as it always has. Men of various ages potter on boats, washing hulls and cleaning portholes.

Modern boatpeople, those who live on boats rather than just holiday on them, are notoriously territorial about the canals. Anyone on any other sort of boat is generally considered an intruder. A bright-red blow-up dinghy might cause a bit of indignation, and I learnt quickly how to spot a boatperson driving, rather than a holidaymaker. If it's a rented boat, you cling to anything you can grab because renters tend not to be great drivers. If it's a boatperson, you have to adopt an apologetic air and make sure you're very much to the right of their boat, which, as Dave had reminded me, is the accepted rule of passing. You certainly shouldn't look curious, as then you become merely a floating gongoozler.

So, a boatyard full of boatpeople might have been a little intimidating, but as I navigated through I was greeted with lots of surprised but warm hellos. I had entered a hidden world, and that I was bold enough to take myself there seemed enough for the gang. An industrial-sized fire pit burned furiously, and from a certain angle you could see the peak of the Buddhist Peace Pagoda in the park, its brilliant golden dome adding to the surreality of the scene.

Through the bridge hole the other side of the boatyard, the world was deserted again. The only access to the canal by foot was via the back of the Icknield glassworks, majestic behind the tumbledown broken windows in the canal wall. On the other side of the canal there was a working factory. Out of it came a low, long, deep boom, followed by some clattering and banging, then another boom. It was an unsettling rhythm – the sound of a giant throwing a car, then rattling the shattered pieces to pick out what was inside.

Up against the side of the glassworks, the old hulls of once-working boats were moored. Some were a modern version of a 'day' or 'joey' boat, open-topped vessels made from steel, used for short-haul work. There was no cabin space and no protection in them – they were like trailers. They were mostly used for coal and other bulky goods: a simple metal hull with a rudder that could hang from either end so that the boat would not need turning. At first they were pulled by horses, later towed by tugs. These great hunks of metal sit all along the Birmingham Canal Network. They have filled with rain-water, debris and their own strange ecology, like little ponds floating in the water.

I tied the boat to the end of one and, trying not to be too unsettled by the booming factory noise, climbed on top of it. Inside, a buoyancy aid was floating near some flag irises and a lone water dock, which seemed to love its watery conditions: it was handsome and majestic in a way that water dock plants rarely are.

I sat on the prow and took in the rest of that stretch. I saw a dozen or so butterflies basking, fighting or taking flight to land upon the blooms of Oregon grape. There were birch, crack willow, blackthorn and various dead nettles. There was waste everywhere, too, old bits of machinery, more broken glass, barbed wire, and that ominous boom, but as I basked in the sun on the warmth of the metal hull, it was just too lovely to notice that.

4

Days later, the backwaters of that loop fascinated me. At night, I dreamt of returning to it, swimming, running through the water or just floating back down the same stretch that runs after the boatyard. In those dreams I saw everything in great detail.

Nothing in that stretch was precious, not the abandoned day boats, the rubbish strewn in the water, the wayside weeds or the framed views of the urban wasteland beyond the broken factory façades. Nature there was a mixture of native and non-native. The weeds were growing straight out of heavy-metal pollution and were stunted or burnt by the effort. None of the trees showed the soft, new green of spring, but instead were flushed already with deficiencies, their trunks scarred by the battles of living there, their branches strewn with ribbons of plastic. As I returned to those images, I was already obsessed with and a little haunted by that landscape. I went back to do the loop again.

It was as unsettled as I was. Its position was as temporal as mine. It was barely holding itself together: the canal sides were crumbling, the banks bursting with wild things ready to march into the water and claim new ground. That landscape couldn't quite decide what it was. It was wild, but not natural, it was old, but not old enough. Its riches kept changing or floating away. It belonged only to those who cared to claim it, outsiders, tenacious wildlife, the drunken, the homeless, the lost and me.

I had never been much for joining in or up. I liked people and I liked belonging, but I have always floated between identities. One foot here, the other there, ready to move on if the boundaries seem to be settling into something rigid. I like best the edges of society, of ecosystems, of friendships. I like the place that is both held onto and departs from. And this watery world was just that. For the first time in nine years, I'd found a bit of Birmingham to fall for and all my internal butterflies took flight with excitement.

I felt the great pull of the unknown, of adventure, setting in: if a place that was just a few miles from the city centre could hold another world so strange and unsettled, what would the rest reveal? The pastoral edges of the network didn't pull me half as much as the dirty great industrial heart and its drum-thumping factories.

*   *   *

At the end of the Icknield Loop I realised I was famished. One of the unexpected joys of an urban adventure is eating. Sure, there's no romance of campfire cooking, but instead there's a city of restaurants to sample. I've wandered in dripping canal water to eat Greek wraps, filled with garlicky roasted vegetables and topped with fluffy, finely fried homemade chips. I've fuelled routes with a quick espresso of freshly roasted Bolivian beans, and ended other adventures with a hoppy jar of craft beer and a round of pickles before the bus home. That I smelt of canal water, was carrying a paddle and half dead with exhaustion seemed to faze none of my servers. This time, though, I had friends to see.

I paddled down to the roundabout and headed for Aston until the first of the Farmer's Bridge locks, where I deflated the boat, then ran across town to catch lunch.

*   *   *

Sarah, Ming and Charlotte forged their friendship on the Birmingham queer scene and had navigated onwards to an old, settled friendship. Charlotte was up from London on a rare visit for lunch. I sat at the edge of their world and listened to them catch up on a wide circle of friends. Charlotte and I knew each other through work: she is a landscape designer. We'd found we had a shared love of hill walking and agreed to tackle an Irish mountain once the project was over. Sarah was Charlotte's first girlfriend, many, many moons ago. I guess, thanks to social networks on the internet, we realised we all knew each other. In retrospect I'm not sure I was invited to that lunch, I think I might have crashed it, but nobody seemed to mind.

Ming and Sarah have been together for twenty years. Ming de Nasty is an ex-punk from Telford, a photographer, a mushroom hunter and amateur taxidermist, a collector of small animal skulls, an allotment-tender, a gardener, and a spotter of fine logs and intricate barks. The daughter of a Shropshire dairy farmer, she reminds me of good country folk, an earthy, no-nonsense, slightly eccentric, open-hearted, non-judgemental lover of the world outside. Just thinking of Ming makes me smile.

And Sarah, gentle, soft, kind Sarah: that's how I think of her. Thoughtful and philosophical Sarah – I can talk about everything and anything with her. Sarah was born in Birmingham but grew up in Essex. Her mum is from Jamaica and her dad is English. She works with young people, often those who have fallen between the gaps, teaching them how to make music. I guess, to a lot of people, she looks a little like a teenage boy. She climbs much better than a boy, being an accomplished boulderer. She's curious and her curiosity takes her everywhere, has her exploring and climbing into every nook and cranny, whether that's the far reaches of your brain or a disused building. She is one of life's great adventurers.

After we were fed and watered, Charlotte suggested we go back down to the canals and paddle the boat. Sarah, it turned out, had been trying to persuade Ming they should get an inflatable boat. It seemed the perfect excuse to show off my beautiful red dinghy.

As we negotiated our route to the water, I heard their version of Birmingham. Here was the street where they'd lost a car, there a night in jail, around this corner there was a minor dispute about how long one had worked there before she dumped the other. These roads were full of dancing.

The best maps are not published, are not accurate or even sensible, but are the maps we make ourselves, about our cities, towns, villages and landscapes, our kith and kin. They are made up of private details that allow us to navigate our past as well as our current terrain. We all make these maps, filled with personal detail. Here's the corner I realised I was in love, there I was happy, here I lost my bike, and over there, I caught the scent of an ex-lover, then had to sit down and cry. The sight of that long vista always saves my soul – a private tapestry of my turf.

My maps are mostly made up of plants. I don't navigate by street names: here is my favourite city oak; outside the dole office, an almond always gives nuts to those prepared to hunt; that is where my favourite urban dandelion once poked its head out. I can forage in that corner for garlic or damsons or the seed of opium poppies.

There is a corner of London's East Village where my heart was broken. To this day I feel it crack whenever I walk along that pavement. Kew Bridge still makes my heart leap – it's where I realised I was in love with my husband. There is a dark, mossy, fern-laden gorge in Ireland, and a corner of a community garden in Manhattan that both have pieces of my heart or, at least, its muscle memory, safe for when I need to give it away again in the future.

I took Ming, Sarah and Charlotte to Farmer's Bridge under Snow Hill train tracks to play and paddle beneath its cathedral-like arch. I forced them to go to the middle and whistle loudly to hear the echo that's only audible to someone floating away from the edge. Ming told us of coracle adventures, and by the end, Charlotte was soaked. For an hour or so, we played like children do: we messed around, we explored, we teased, we were aimless; we conquered banks and weirs. Everyone who passed was drawn into the strange spectacle we made. We met a man who had scuba-dived to the bottom of the canal to help fix a lock in the sixties, 'but I'd never swim in them now, mind'. I thought he'd probably got that the wrong way round: they're far cleaner now than ever before. And another who had decided his wife would love such a boat: would I take him through the intricacies of blowing it up? We met cyclists and more curious gongoozlers. Soon it was time to put Charlotte on a train home to London.

Having company around the boat was rather pleasing, and within a week, Ming and Sarah had bought their own inflatable canoe. As someone who had spent a lovely, if lonely, childhood, with only wild things for friends, I'm still thrilled by adult friendship. Now I had the beginning of a boat gang.

* * *

Often I think that living with cystic fibrosis – or, for that matter, any long-term chronic illness – is a little like climbing a mountain. Mountains are beautiful, resolute and often difficult places. They are there to teach us our limits and our possibilities. They are there for us to get lost on and find ourselves. Anything and everything can change with the whips of the weather on a mountain. One crag can be calm with warm zephyrs, and around the corner the wind is raging. You can never be entirely certain of how the terrain will behave. You can always be caught out, but if you're lucky, you get to the top and have a view of this world that alters everything. You get to stand and see where you've come from and where you will go.

I had learnt to live with cystic fibrosis as the third other in our marriage. It changed everything and nothing. It was always present, often hidden, momentarily forgotten or so subsumed into life that we didn't notice it. As H's carer, I had duties, but they were hardly onerous, and they didn't feel a burden because I loved my husband's company. Although I also love my independence and time alone, I turned out to be very suited to companionship. I loved being married. It felt freeing, perhaps because I had found someone who loved solitude and being absorbed in their work as much as I did.

So, between writing and gardening, I cooked, I cleaned, I picked up medication when needed, I visited hospitals for appointments, for stays. Mostly my biggest duty was to worry, and that was a choice, though sometimes it didn't feel so.

I had also learnt to be a little circumspect around the details. There is a lot of judgement around disability. It's not often mean or meant to be so, but it's there. I had learnt to hate having to tell people about H's condition because then I went from being an ordinary married woman to being in a place of pity. I know we both hated that. But not to talk of it was also to silence an important difference. No, we are not like you, but we are also just like you. One of the harsh realities of life's problems is that they are all relative. On paper, mine may be bigger or smaller than yours, but when you're stuck in the eye of the storm of a problem, whether it's debt, loneliness, sickness or greed, there's the same looming, somewhat terrifying mountain to climb.

Faced with that mountain, I'd do the only thing I knew to try to steady my world. I'd sink into nature. Mostly I'd sink into the smallest part I could find. I started with the world at my feet. I'd take my magnifying hand lens and examine the fine feathery scales of young moss. I'd take dead bees and observe their furry stomachs. I'd peel back the bark on punk wood to hunt for slime moulds, and peer into the centre of flowers to look at pollen. I'd push my fingers into warm earth and soft, rotting woods, and cling to the very small all around me. I'd walk the same path every day so I could note the smallest change.

Then, when I felt steadier, I'd start to look up. I'd climb trees to hide among their boughs. I'd be so very quiet and hidden that nature flooded over me and I'd find extraordinary peace as all the molecules in my body sighed back to the places they'd come from. I'd stare at the ground, I'd stare just above, and when I felt ready, I'd finally look up and outwards, ready to take it on again. I repeated this endlessly, and it always worked. A very small world, though, can only sustain so much. If you refuse to take in the horizon, the world below your feet will always become dizzying. I started to want to bolt. It rose up in me when I least expected it, and I had to use all of my energy to hold that hollow feeling at the top of my stomach and not let it near my heart.

I needed to get away to a place where I could be left alone. My tiny world under my feet, through the woodland to the allotment, had become very populated with people. When I started on my overgrown plot, nothing much more was said than a grunt. And when I'd pulled my own plot into order and started to garden the spare bits, to plant bulbs in lawns and roses under windows, I suddenly wasn't alone. There was much to be said and many people to say things to. My allotment is my community. I began to realise that time alone in nature was what I needed most. It's my reset button. It's how I make sense of my world. Stumbling on the world of canals, having a map of where to go, not only made sense, it was inviting, had a whiff of adventure and guaranteed a little solitude.

Out in the middle of the canal it seemed that no one could intrude, and I'd found a wild bit with an unknown horizon in front of me, a place to explore. I had an immediate future that I wanted to run to. It was such a compelling sensation to feel free again.

I'd find myself straining out of train windows to see the canals, noting new routes and underpasses that might be good to explore. In idle moments, in meetings or at home, I dreamt of the boat, the song of the paddle. I started to plan my weeks not by work or tending seedlings, but by when I'd next get down to the water, that dark water, that other world.

My husband turned to me as I rolled up the boat, already in

a frenzy to get out there, and mocked gently, 'You're finding yourself on the canals, aren't you?' I looked preposterous in a beaten-up old felt trilby, with my canvas rucksack spilling paddle parts, clutching my bus money and my crumpled, still-damp map of the canals.

'I'll be back in three hours,' I called. I wouldn't, though, not back as he knew it or as I did. It wasn't the water, the paddle or a new flora to ponder at, but a map that was changing within me.

5

I didn't want to lose time travelling to the canal, so I jumped on the number fifty out to Druid's Heath and was on the water after three stops. This is not a pretty part of town: it's a little rough, not quite posh enough to be part of the 'burbs of Kings Norton, not quite close enough to be metropolitan. It's the land of new-builds and cul-de-sacs. Many of the beige seventies houses have gardens that back onto the canal. There is a certain vernacular to those canal-side patios. There are Jolly Roger flags and pirate forts, there are *faux*-Renaissance balconies, ramshackle builds from driftwood and plastic, and spick-and-span neat versions. There are fortresses against floods, fishing perches and miniature beer gardens.

Few are inhabited at this time of day, though I met a beekeeper further down the canal. All his hives were placed so that the bees take flight straight onto the water, their entrances carefully cut out of his wooden fence. What forage they have there! We talked shop about the coming season and what I should do about the giant population inside my hive that I am terrified will swarm while I'm off paddling. All the while his bees buzzed idly around this new introduction to their waterside world. Stand or boat in front of social bees' – honey or bumble – flight path and you will always get a response.

Guard bees will buzz around you, often at your eyes, nose, mouth and ears, which evolution has taught them are tender spots. If you don't move away, they may even fly straight at you and bounce off as a warning. Stay too long after that and a small army of defenders will be ready to attack if necessary. Honey bees die when they sting; bumbles do not. But in a strange mortality twist, bumbles are actually very hard to anger. They do a lot of posturing, mostly on their backs, showing you their sting, as if to say, 'Really, you want this?' Certain types are more likely to bite than sting you. Honeys, however, are always willing to sacrifice themselves for the colony.

Stand or boat to the side of the entrance and flight path, and you can linger far longer, though eventually a bee will notice you. Often they're just curious to know if you're a new landmark to note. Bees navigate by large, easily distinguished features: a big red boat would be a good one, if it stayed long enough, or at least one to note if the terrain was changing, but I floated past slowly and the task of supper was more pressing to the bees.

It's easy to understand why everyone wants a view over the canal. The waters may be murky but the view beyond is a pastoral idyll. The banks were a riot of spring, hawthorns bursting, feral flowering currants, *Rubus sanguineum*, with thick tassels of pink flowers, a whole bank of wood anemone followed by carpets of celandine, glossy yellow in the afternoon sun.

Everywhere I found trees perfect for swings, the tall banks a great launch for a thrilling ride across the water. There was boat traffic to negotiate, but not enough to interrupt an afternoon of dangerous dangling over the canal. My childhood was full of such swings over streams and, far more terrifying, over railway lines. Why were those trees empty of ropes and log-fashioned seats? In the coming days I would find a great length of nylon rope in our attic and squirrel it into my boat bag for the next suitable tree.

Below those leaning trees, some oaks, many alders or willows, there was a hidden lapping world of crevices and hollows where the dappled sun turned the water amber. I've always loved those fairy spaces, the entry into another world. My mother used to tell me that the hollows between surface roots, which filled with rainwater, were where the fairies came to bathe. You were never allowed to say you didn't believe in fairies in her household, lest you killed one. To this day, my mother stands by her word that others live in this world. There, at the edge of the bank, I imagined the fairy boatpeople floating on craft fashioned from our rubbish, a boat from a plastic water bottle, a submarine from a beer can, a sail made from a carrier bag. I peered deep into one of the holes and came to my senses: the only little people down those tunnels were rats. Water rats, not voles, nothing quite so cute and enchanting, big fat, furtive rats that swam in the slick, slimy water impervious to the pollution.

I was distracted from those dark thoughts by a rhythmic engine noise, a lovely sound, its warm song racing through the water. I saw an ancient working narrowboat, with space for carrying cargo, a beautiful vintage engine and, behind it, a butty boat. The sides of the working boat were covered with tarps that could be rolled up or down to protect the cargo. The engine room was partially exposed, and from it issued the burnished brass chimney pipe, with a great plume of white smoke. In front of the engine sat a pile of neatly chopped logs. The boat was painted a deep sky blue and the hull was tarred black. It was a vessel of great beauty, driven by a tall, good-looking young man in a thick, old-fashioned wool coat. He had dark hair, dark eyes and olive skin, slightly gaunt, and we stared at each other, only just acknowledging that we might be a strange sight to each other.

The butty boat, being towed behind it, was the living quarters. Behind the handmade curtains, you could see a lovely interior, a row of hanging mugs, a washing-up bowl – a carefully crafted space. At the stern, guiding the great swan-like neck of the wooden helm, a young woman stood in a long skirt and a thick woolly jumper, mug steaming in one hand, the other guiding the tiller. A boy sat on top of the cabin, reading aloud to his mother. He had a sort of school uniform on, with long socks and wool shorts, and an equally thick old jumper. The whole fantastically handsome family was perfectly curated to the decade of their boat. The thick sweaters, the ancient mugs and the polished brass are not things you inherit but piece together. Time stood still while they ploughed past to their own rhythmic song. I half wanted to follow them, to ask them about their ways and wants, but their engine was far faster than my arms, and I sensed they were perfectly self-sufficient in their fashioned ways.

I placed my paddle on the bow of my boat and spun around in their wake listening to their engine till I could hear it no longer. Then, realising I was drifting backwards fast, I took up the paddle and worked hard through the water to make up time. I was heading for a tunnel.

Before I went inside, I spent a good few minutes reading the instructions for entering in a 'non-powered' craft. I couldn't meet the requirements so I texted Dave and asked his advice. Dutifully, he went to some rulebook and said it was not advisable to go in without a head torch, which I didn't possess, but I could see light at the end of the tunnel so I decided to ignore that. I should have learnt that ignoring instructions to do with boats is unwise, but I'm not very good on the fine print in life.

At 322 metres, the Brandwood Tunnel is long enough to be intimidating. It has no towpath and is just big enough to allow two boats to pass through. Traditionally in such tunnels the horse would have been led over the bridge, while the bargees hauled their boats through, using the handrails. Fragments of those were still visible in places, but once I was inside that dark subterranean world there was little to persuade me that I should touch the edges. The whole tunnel grew a very strange, slimy, bubbly orange mould that dripped endlessly and played tricks with my eyes the darker the tunnel got.

The head torch is necessary to warn oncoming boats that you're in the tunnel but, come the middle, it might also have saved my imagination. The noise of the paddles lingered as the water sucked under some invisible lip and gurgled. As the darkness deepened, I could no longer make out the blades of the paddle and missed the water several times, throwing the boat into a spin. I hit something with the prow and then the paddle. I felt it pass under my boat. The bottom of a pack raft is just a membrane, thin enough that you will feel ripples on the water. Whatever passed under me stroked my legs and sent a chill up my back.

I had passed the middle by now but the light was not brightening, though some strange slime mould made a section of the tunnel glow lime green. I saw more things floating in the water. Out loud, I had to tell myself that no one could live in the tunnel without a towpath. But I couldn't help thinking of some dark, shrouded being climbing up over the prow of the boat. I panicked and missed my stroke, spinning the boat again. I fumbled for my phone and used the torch to check what was in the water. Logs, lots of logs, which must have fallen off a boat passing through, bobbing slowly down a very long tunnel. I felt foolish and paddled on.

The arch at the end of the tunnel seemed no closer. Suddenly cold water gushed down the back of my neck. I couldn't imagine where so much could have come from and paddled manically until I reached the real world. Later I read that all long tunnels have air vents and that the sudden rush of water was run-off from above ground, draining through this vent.

The other side of the tunnel was beautiful. The bridge curved with a circular plaque just above the voussoirs, which hold up an arch. By the time I came out, I had found a new passion, the art of arch-building, and spent an evening learning about its intricacies.

The plaque contained a crumbling bust, but it was not readily identifiable as anyone in particular other than another balding man. Later I discovered that the bridge was built in the late eighteenth century by Josiah Clowes and was the gateway to Stratford-upon-Avon, while the eroded bust is of the Bard. Essentially, it's an escape tunnel from industrial gloom. No wonder it's only pretty going out, with Shakespeare to wave you on.

The whole arch swept outwards and ended in a frill of beech leaves. It was quite something for a portal in the suburbs. I slowly spun around in the boat, admiring the detail, the fine red bricks, and the theatre of it all, hidden from the rumbling traffic above.

All at once I heard an engine and a boat appeared around the corner going full pelt, its driver caring little that the wake was washing me into branches. We glared at each other and I was grateful that I'd made it out of the tunnel before he appeared. I shuddered at the thought of what might have happened had I not. It had been reckless to go through in the dark. Mentally I added a back-and-front head torch and perhaps even a horn to my kitbag. The next tunnel I'd have to negotiate would be almost two miles long. Still, I knew I had to do a lot more paddling before my arms would be strong enough to tackle that.

The rest of the journey to Stirchley was peppered with pretty architectural features. The Kings Norton Junction Toll House was once the canal's headquarters. For years it had been in a somewhat dishevelled state, the garden in particular in complete disarray, although the house looked as if someone was now living in it. It has lovely Doric columns around the door and, like many who pass it, I fancied living there.

Another pretty little brick bridge was followed by the rather terrifying Guillotine Lock, which stopped Birmingham canal water flowing into the Stratford Canal. Water was owned by various canal bodies: the Birmingham Canal Network was separate from the Stratford Canal, and as water had a price, no one wanted to lose theirs to the competitor. The fifteen-centimetre difference in heights between the Birmingham Canal Network and the Stratford Canal was not enough to require a traditional lock to move the boats, which would have been very expensive to build, just enough for the owners not to want to lose that water. With a guillotine lock, a wooden board is lifted to let the boat pass, then sent back down quickly to prevent any more movement of water. It makes a strong statement about stealing water, I guess.

That lock is permanently open, these days, but the gate

framework is beautiful cast iron. The gate is hand-winched, using a counterweight chain mechanism. There are plenty of tales of such gates going wrong and landing straight down on boats. Once the canals were nationalised, stealing water was no longer an issue, so the gates started to rot from underuse and thus lived up to their name. There aren't many left now so it's worth pausing for a good gander if you're passing one.

The rest of the journey was less picturesque as industry started to play its drum: an old brick factory, with suitably fine walls and windows to the canal. Then came a bank of unfurling butterbur, strange ancient flowers, like a grove of miniature pale trees. I saw many wary geese, sitting on fragile nests of down, feathers and plastic bags, and a few posturing males. The ganders actually do a lot of nesting and are far more ferociously protective than the geese. A goose on the towpath is not that intimidating. However, a gander swimming next to a slow-paddling human is fully aware of its superior position and I was chased down the canal until I was far enough away to be no longer a threat. I turned to see the gander bobbing its long, strong neck, like a boxer dancing in the ring between bouts. The roots of weedy alders crept into the water and a small but curious gang of crows, each bending its head as I passed by, kar-kar-karing in unison.

As I entered Stirchley I could smell paint fumes and melted plastic and suddenly felt very tired. I hauled myself out onto a grassy bank and packed up as quickly as I could. There was a hike of a mile or so up a hill to home and lunch.

6

Sarah and Ming bought a boat within a week of floating about in mine and we planned a joint expedition. I would paddle up from the university and meet them at the basin, and from there we would do the Oozell Street Loop to see the Boatyard and end at the Round House, a restored narrowboat yard and pub, for supper.

I left myself two hours to get from home to town. It's around three miles from the university into town, a stretch of water that is shadowed by the railway line – all the way up you have a soundtrack of train announcements. All along the canal there are towering banks with sandy slopes, huge old oaks and tall graceful beeches. I also spotted many mining bee colonies: tiny holes in sunny, sandy places where each bee tunnels a home and lays her eggs. They looked like condos, the holes so numerous and regular. Every now and then, a female darted out to find new material to build her brood's home. It's a lovely rural stretch and for that reason the towpath is well used by walkers, joggers and cyclists. I attracted plenty of curious onlookers, including a young man, who videoed me for slightly too long. In the end I felt so observed that I plugged my phone into my ears to blast away that other world with music.

As I left the university campus, I came across a young dead fox on the side of the towpath. It was so bedraggled that at first I thought it might be a dog, but close up its long tail gave it away.

It was lying on its back as if it had just woken up and had rolled over to bask in the sun. It was a very curious position for a dead animal. I'm not even sure it had died drowning. It looked as if it had been floating along until someone had fished it out.

It was such a strange sight that I stayed with it for some time, took a photo and contemplated dragging it behind the boat for Ming, who is a keen amateur taxidermist. A young man and two young women came past and the girls reacted in horror, skirting around the fox. One screamed. I decided that dragging it behind my boat might not do much for my image and paddled off.

A little further, in the corner of the bridge hole, I found a bloated dead Canada goose, its neck snapped so that its head was now resting on its back. It had the obscene look of anything that has drowned, bloated and buoyant, bobbing around. A pair of pigeons wandered by, totally unfazed by the giant gassy object, the male cooing to his mate, nodding and ruffling his neck feathers. There was something a little sordid about it all – the filth and bad graffiti under the bridge, the stench of the rotting goose, the train honking past, nature red, raw and unbothered by other dead things.

Another bridge on, my eye caught something curious growing on the edge of the bank. A morel mushroom was lying between a young person's railcard and a stolen wallet. There were another two, wilted and rotting back to where they'd come from. I wasn't sure if they were true or false morels. A true morel's cap is joined to the stem, which is hollow; a false morel's cap is not joined and can easily be peeled back. The stem of a false morel also has clear sections if cut open. A false morel will give you a bad stomach-ache. True ones make a fine feast. I couldn't reach the morel and didn't want to uproot it just for identification purposes.

Morels are mainly saprotrophs: they use chemoheterotrophic extracellular digestion. They release a bunch of enzymes into the matter around them to break down their dinner into small enough parts for their fine, thread-like hyphae, a sort of root, to take up. Essentially they liquidise their surroundings and suck them up. This all happens below ground, hidden from the eye. The mushroom on the surface isn't doing any of that, though: it's there to release its spores into the air to find new territory.

Fungi's role in life is to decompose waste matter. Good soil is made by good mushrooms that turn waste into nourishment for other life in the soil. People are terrified of fungi appearing in their garden, but if your soil sprouts unknown mushrooms, be thankful that it's turning something you can't use into something you can. Fungi breaks down the tough stuff, the stuff that wind and rain and bacteria can't weather. Fungi are the only organisms on earth that can decompose dead wood and, for that matter, your toenails. Fungi might save our world, by cleaning up our waste – chemical toxins, oil spills and other contaminants. There are numerous programmes for bioremediation, cleaning up toxic land, which employ fungi to degrade toxic waste, turning it at molecular level from a threat to something more benign. Rather than digging up toxic ground and removing it, fungi can be grown to bring land back to health. Within their lifecycle, they can turn dangerous chemicals into hydrogen, water and carbon dioxide.

But one thing is for sure: however delicious a morel can be, you don't want to eat one growing on any sort of industrial pollution. Bath Row Bridge, where that morel lived, has been at various points a cemetery, Birmingham's first hospital, a brewery and a bit of railway. And, left alone, that mushroom would release spores and start again, going through its cycle until the soil could support something else.

I left it where it was, taking a photograph to prove that foraging in Birmingham was interesting. Then, aware that I might now be very late to meet my friends, I paddled hard, straight up and into the basin. The Mailbox tour-boat owner recognised me instantly, checked that the bend ahead was clear and waved me on. I felt chuffed to be accepted as a canal user and waved my paddle back, perhaps a little too enthusiastically.

Ming and Sarah appeared with their vastly superior boat: an inflatable canoe with a giant pump and fancy seats. It made my little dinghy seem even more laughable. They had been out on one exploratory paddle together, but still hadn't quite agreed on their stroke, so we paddled around while they got into the swing of things. They quickly found a rhythm and it was clear that their boat would cut through the water fast. Mine tracks back and forth like a duck waddling along on land.

My boat has no rudder and no skeg – a small fin that sits under the boat to improve tracking. Skegs are ideal if you canoe, but of little help if you pack-raft. The nature of the boat means that you can't go fast and thus you track, so we went along rather slowly. Alone, I hadn't noticed how slow my boat was, but next to something that slid gracefully through the water, I felt a little ridiculous.

I'd taken to strapping my folding bike onto the prow: this makes the boat heavy so it is also forced to sit lower in the water, which means it waddles less. There is something very pleasing about tiring your arms till they burn with exhaustion, then packing the boat and using your legs to fuel the final journey home.

Despite the odd disagreement about whether they should paddle right or left oar first, Ming and Sarah were naturally very good at it. Ming sat up front, Sarah behind. I couldn't turn to look at them very often because paddling is a bit like riding a bike: if you look in one direction too long you veer off. However, I could hear their gentle banter as they teased each other for losing a stroke or knocking each other off balance. They were particularly easy company and I started to relax into the evening.

I took them up the Icknield Loop to the Boatyard. Work had ended for the day so the yard was deserted. It was deliciously quiet and still and we nosed around in our boats. Down a side pond, I spotted a waterfall and we went to investigate. This was the water from the reservoir that endlessly tops up the canal. It fell over a brutalist structure hidden beneath concrete fittings. Old tyres, twisted metal and bits of cars blocked the way, presumably to stop nosy sorts like us having a look. The water was heavily silted and shallow and thus very warm. We disturbed a heron fishing and he swooped over our heads. In the shallow, slow-moving water, great pike darted about. Perhaps it was their breeding ground. They are known to lay eggs in such conditions.

Once mature, pike are fearsome, happily eating their way through the food chain. They like roach and rudd, frogs, newts and toads, and are partial to baby moorhens and coots, and ducklings. A mature female can grow up to a metre in length and live for twenty years. I once kicked a very large specimen while I was swimming in the Serpentine in London and have never felt such a panic in cold water. Every early-morning Serpentine swimmer has apocalyptic tales of pike that mistook wiggling toes for a tasty catch.

Pike are happy canal creatures adapted to live among the plants' margins, not caring to swim far from their cover. It was thrilling to see them dart under the boats, but the shards of metal were unnerving for inflatable boaters. We gingerly backed our craft past the hazards.

Sarah has city ways. She might have grown up down south, but her teenaged self was formed in Birmingham. She mapped her city by bike and sometimes roller skates, headphones on, around Small Heath parks, working in bars and pubs, running club nights, dancing her way across the city and back again. She also has an in-built sound map to our city, an industrial ear: amid unidentified slag heaps and the anonymous steel façade of factory fronts, the timbre of a bang, the resonance of clatter were all instantly identifiable. When I said that a factory sounded like a banging giant, she dead-panned, 'You mean pressed metal!' The symphony of clangs was just the noise of the industrial incinerator. I hadn't felt like a country mouse in a very long time, but I was fooled by the high banks of beeches and oaks, the dripping bluebell vistas and the garlanded alders thick with wild clematis and ivy. My naïve country self reappeared. One that believed in giants and ogres and fairies under the bridge.

We paddled on to where the old metal hulls of working boats were moored up. Some were sinking, others were floating ponds and a few were empty. We tied up our boats and explored them. Then we decided to explore behind the factory wall where there was an expanse of rubble and wild plants, mostly coltsfoot, buddleja seedlings, ragwort and birch saplings among the factory remnants.

We gently quizzed each other about Charlotte. How I knew her, how she knew them. Charlotte and I, of course, had worked together on the park I'd helped to design in London, another area in my professional life. I sometimes wish there was a job title for what I do. The only common thread is plants: I write, I present, I design, I teach, I garden. So I knew Charlotte professionally, but now I was hanging about with her, and they were rightly curious. I was curious too. I liked new people. I liked Charlotte. I liked Ming and Sarah. I liked the possibilities of new relationships.

I knew Ming and Sarah because I worked with their best friends at the BBC, but I sat on the edge of that friendship. And Ming and I had so much in common in terms of our gardening passion that it was a little odd that it had taken us so long to hang out. I guess that was partly why I was so pleased that she and Sarah wanted to come out paddling: it seemed a good opportunity to get to know them better.

We left the disused factory ground and paddled on to the Soho Loop. I was exhausted: I'd done nearly five miles and my arms had nothing left. We called it a day and paddled back into town to have supper in the Fiddle and Bone, an old pub next to a boatyard that had recently been restored. The food wasn't great, but I was so hungry that I was happy to eat anything and wolfed down a burger with lots of hoppy beer.

* * *

I'd been convinced that I would explore the canals alone. I'd thought it was best as a single activity: two boats would be noisy. I was after solitude, time on my own, but before I knew it, Sarah, Ming and I had made plans for another exploration. Although

I told myself that this was extracurricular and that I was still a lone adventurer, this was just a little socialising, I was thrilled to hang out with them. They loved the water and paddling. They loved nature, and were as keen as I was to explore the wilder margins, to go looking for fabled Birmingham beach, to see if we could find the otters that were supposed to hang out under the motorways. I liked Ming and Sarah a lot. I liked that they liked me. I liked hanging out with women, with those adventurous, funny women, who loved each other so clearly.

7

On May bank holiday Monday, Sarah, Ming and I met at the Ackers, an adventure park you can see as you arrive from London on the Chiltern railway line. There's a go-karting circuit and a brightly coloured playground, and the largest graffitied penis you can imagine, a truly strange bit of urban landscape. We parked and unloaded our boats. The idea was to find the point where the River Rea passed under the canal and see if we could explore it.

We headed off in the wrong direction. We passed some young Muslim men fishing, who laughingly warned us of the Small Heath shark that basked in the warm factory water, a terrible urban myth if ever there was one. We passed some bank-holiday bike riders and met another group of men fishing. We heard them talk in low voices in what I thought might be Romanian. They were taking a fish off one of their lines with a flash of green as it went into a plastic bag. When we asked them what it was they were furtive and cagey about their catch. A tench, perhaps, or carp. They wouldn't show us, perhaps because they thought we would tell them off. Everything you catch in a canal you must return to the water. Eastern Europeans sometimes fish in the canals to eat their catch. The young boy with them smiled shyly. Their British counterparts came with stools and flags, endless rods and nets, sometimes radios and newspapers. In comparison this lot looked very casual. Their rods were short and light, and they wandered up and down as they fished. I guessed necessity had made them itinerant anglers.

Dave later told me that there is great ill feeling towards the eastern Europeans because they often eat their catch. There is good reason not to eat it – the water is so polluted – but poverty surely plays a part. Some people argue that returning the fish protects the ecosystem, but I don't think catching the biggest is bad: it makes room for more. I think there's a degree of snobbery here among the fishing community. British people don't eat carp because they are bony. Likewise you don't often hear of people eating pike. However, in Europe they are desirable fish. The unease between the two groups may also stem from jealousy. The eastern Europeans fish in a very different manner: they are urgent, explorative, endlessly casting and casting again. They hunt: they are not there to lose the day, their pursuit is not a hobby. Theirs is driven by something much more primeval: hunger.

We carried on, leaving the anglers with quiet waters. Some fishermen hate the disturbance of boats. Others say it churns up the water, moving the fish about. I wondered about the flash of green in the plastic bag. Perhaps it was some kind of carp. I'd bought an illustrated book on freshwater fish in the UK from a second-hand bookshop, thinking there was a single type of carp. It turned out there are many and they can interbreed. I liked the look of the leather carp, which is scale-free.

You can't search for fish when there are two boats: the water needs to be very still and quiet. You can't even talk much unless you're just floating. The boats need to be very close together and you have to be going fairly slowly or the paddle drowns your voices. We shouted to each other and pointed out things that pleased us. I often paddled ahead, only to be leisurely overtaken by their more powerful, elegant boat.

* * *

I'd climbed Benbulben in Sligo with Charlotte the weekend before. I say climbed, it was more a leisurely walk onto a high grassy plateau, with a terrifying sheer north face and views over to Donegal. It was a majestic weekend of blue skies, cold swimming and catching up with Irish friends. It was a strange thing to do because Charlotte and I didn't know each other well – I'd thought that walking up a mountain might be a good way to get to know her. I'd also thought that at the top of the mountain we'd know if the walk down was going to be tortuous or not. But I was a little quiet about all those things. Going to Ireland always felt a little like bolting out of real life. I felt restored by it, topped up with green, but a little unsure of how to come back to my life.

* * *

We paddled on, under a bridge or two and out into the suburbs. It felt so very rural there – huge towering banks of beech and oak, thick carpets of Spanish bluebells, glimpses of allotments, golf courses and parks. Sarah spotted a bicycle wheel floating near a rather lovely Victorian sink that was acting as a drainage channel for a bank and declared the wheel hub a perfect match for one of her mountain bikes. She fished it out and strapped it on the back of their boat. We continued all the way down to Acocks Green, to the edge of the city, then decided it was time to head home. The last stretch started to take it out of me and they kindly towed me along, making butch jokes and teasing me as I was dragged backwards. It was welcome respite for a quarter of a mile or so.

Then we met a Polish man, who shouted that he was starting up a 'Polish barbecue'. I asked what was for supper, half hoping for an invitation, but he shook his head and said it was just 'Polish meat'. It was a friendly exchange, though we were all left to wonder what Polish meat was. I liked the unofficial canal-side life. The plastic chairs perched outside factories for a peaceful fag break, the endless buddleja forests, the shanty-town verandas perhaps with a pot for flowers, a pit for barbecuing or just a place to rest. My safe, slightly boring city was different on the canals: there, it was a little subversive, a little less structured; it had something that was missing from the gentrified bits. With little monetary value, anyone could define or claim those backwaters. Ownership was still a loose term there, and it reminded me of why I'd landed in Birmingham, half by mistake, quite sure I'd have gone back to London within a few months. I'd rooted myself there now, like a buddleja in a wall. It would be hard to extract myself. Birmingham was home.

*   *   *

Buddleja, you are a crack addict. I remember thinking as a child that an old wild one I knew would be good to climb, all those opposing branches like a twisting ladder perfect for my small feet. I swung myself about the bush, arched branches cracking, throwing me here and there, until I'd broken them into a battered petticoat and landed hard on my arse on stony ground. I remember the noise of the final crack and the thud that took my breath clean away and stung long after.

It grew in the chicken yard and was allowed to remain, I think, only because it brought butterflies and perhaps because the chickens didn't eat it, although they often scrambled into it. My mother is crazy for butterflies. In a dressing room upstairs, in the bottom drawer of a huge old wardrobe, there was a tin box full of tiny triangles of faded newspaper: they contained thousands of specimens, wings folded shut for ever. If you tried to prise them apart, the wings shattered into iridescent fragments, leaving just the hairy bodies denuded and alien. My mother had collected them in Africa and someone had taught her the careful fold of the newspaper so that you could bring them home and mount them. She had never learnt to do that and, shut tight too long, there was no spell to open this magic book. She felt embarrassed and saddened for the flight of imagination she had failed to display. She said she should not have collected them in the first place, but once she had she should at least have prised them open again. I wonder what distracted her.

Buddleja was not a plant to which I paid attention. It had no good countryside qualities. You couldn't climb it, you couldn't eat it, you couldn't hide in it particularly well. No one was impressed if you picked it for them. It didn't make a decent sword, and you couldn't whittle it into anything much. The pith in the middle of the older fissured branches was fun to dig your nails into, but even that pleasure didn't last long, and although the flowers smelt sweet, there were other much more exciting things to sniff.

I remember being twenty-one or so, sitting on a window ledge off the kitchen of a boyfriend's flat and noticing it properly for the first time. *Buddleja davidii*, the butterfly-bush, weed of the wayside. Why did you end up in a crack? And why do you choose to live there now? You have the choice of so many places to grow, yet you still choose your crack. Why do you like it so?

There are three places where you will always find *Buddleja davidii* in cities: in cracks; on embankments; by water. There are three places you will find *Buddleja davidii* growing in the wild: on limestone outcrops; in forest clearings; as a riverside thicket.

Buddleja davidii was introduced into Europe in 1893 and its showy flowers made it a firm favourite with the Victorians, especially the burgeoning middle class. Buddleja flowers are loved by butterflies, whose long proboscises can explore the deep reaches of the long corolla tube of those lovely little flowers. The deep orange eye is a nectar guide, the heavenly honey scent a seductive attractant, and the thin, sweet, abundant nectar a delight for a long slender tongue to sup up. Butterflies are wild for buddlejas, basking on those dense masses of panicles that flower from late spring to autumn, each flower lasting no more than three days, but from the first bloom at the bottom to the last at the tip the whole ca-boom can last up to two weeks. A feast indeed. The flowers are upright to help the pollinators, and when their work is done the seed is easily dispersed by the wind. So, all those Victorian specimens made a bid for a wilder life, but it was not until the 1930s that buddleja made a jail break and won. There were very few noted escapes prior to 1935.

In the 1930s buddleja began to colonise limestone quarries. Old walls and areas of exposed chalk land quickly become buddleja settlements too. These are to the buddleja ideal habitats; a home from home. The expanding rail network provided a similar dwelling: a railway embankment is not a million miles away from a forest clearing, and is also a means of further seed dispersal. The locomotive slipstream is a charged wind, which spreads those seeds, the gravel and rock of the railway sides another limestone outcrop to embrace. The Second World War provided further homes: bombed buildings, rich in lime mortar, and rubble offered yet more space for buddleja to naturalise. And perhaps from sentimentality for the plant that had softened the heartache of a post-war city, or even because they require no effort on the part of the owner, the buddleja was embraced in the 1950s and 1960s as a popular garden plant.

Buddleja went from domestic to feral in just three decades. Follow the map of its spread, and the country went from a sparse few dots to blanketed with it in no time at all.

Our pollinators are declining for many reasons – a cocktail of chemicals, in the form of pesticides and fungicides, a lack of nesting and resting habitats and a decline in food sources, which, most importantly, aren't covered with a cocktail of chemicals. Buddleja, then, represents a huge chemical-free resource for butterflies and bees. It may grow where it's undesired, but the results are very desirable indeed.

8

Finally Dave and I got to go on an adventure in our boats. We hadn't been paddling together since my first venture onto the water, although we had chewed the fat about this trip for some time. In fact, it's safe to say that all we'd talked about since I'd started the water lark was canals. He'd text me with funny canal facts or send me black-and-white clips of yesteryear's canals, and technical drawings of locks. Very early on in all the plotting and planning he declared that my adventure needed a peak to aim for: the Dudley Tunnel. Then he regaled me with tales of how it was built and how difficult it was to gain access to. I had read that to go through it now you either had to own a pre-1930 narrowboat, the only ones small enough to get through, or to persuade the Dudley Canal Trust to let you paddle it. At two miles long, with no towpath, no lighting, and so deep beneath the earth that there's no mobile-phone reception, once you're in that tunnel you really are out of contact with this world. It sounded fantastic and a little terrifying.

I rang the Trust, and they were surprisingly amenable to my request, asking only that Dave and I go through the tunnel with one of their electric narrowboats following in case we got stuck. That, and a donation to the Trust. We agreed a date on which I could paddle and I put the phone down in a slight daze. Then I called Dave, who, within a heartbeat, was making plans to join me.

After my last somewhat hallucinatory tunnel experience, I was glad I'd have company. Two miles, deep in the belly of the earth: it was not a journey I was quite ready to do alone.

*   *   *

The Dudley Tunnel was officially opened to traffic in 1792. It was built in part to provide access to the limestone caverns under Castle Hill, which were formed some time in the pre-history of the Silurian Age, some 400 million years ago, when the first moss-like plants were colonising Earth. Dudley and its mines are some of the best examples of this geological period in the world, not that you'd have any idea of it if you skirted past it on the motorway, but perhaps that's part of its charm.

By the eighteenth century, the caves had become an important part of the Black Country industrial revolution, the limestone being essential for removing impurities in the smelting of iron ore. It is said that the Lord Dudley and Ward might have paid for the tunnel, but the people of Dudley paid the price. Many miners and canal builders, some of them children as young as nine years old, lost their lives either down in that subterranean world or barely out of it. The lack of vitamin D from six days a week down in the dark caused countless cases of rickets and other diseases.

The tunnel is two miles long with no towpath. Initially bargees would have pushed the boats through using poles, but the cheap bricks start to disintegrate and the Dudley Canal Company declared they would not spend money on replacing bricks. From then on the bargees had to lie on their backs on top of their cabins and push their feet against the roof, 'legging' the boat down the tunnel. You can still see where hundreds of feet have pushed at the ceiling. Shifting up to thirty tons of boat with just your legs is a crazy feat. I did about fifteen feet with the Trust's unloaded electric boat, weighing about fifteen tonnes, and could barely stand up at the end.

In 1858, the Netherton Tunnel was built. It was a superior tunnel, wider, higher and, with twin towpaths, a horse could draw the boats along. It also had gas lighting that was later replaced with electric lights powered by a nearby water turbine. This tunnel outstripped demand, and although the Dudley Tunnel was in use until the Second World War, over time traffic gradually decreased. It was saved from permanent closure in the 1970s by some enthusiasts and is open now to those bold enough to ask.

The day we decided to tackle the Dudley Tunnel was hot and bright, and our inflatable boats expanded quickly as the air inside warmed. I worried that mine might pop, and released a little air before we went in. That was a mistake: halfway through the tunnel the middle began to sag. I prayed it wouldn't go down any more before the end. The water has a strange smell, not wholly natural yet not fetid, just forgotten perhaps.

To get to the Dudley Tunnel you must first go through a much shorter one. That was a breeze to paddle and we came out into a collapsed mine with great curtains of ivy at least twenty feet long, covering various smaller caverns that had been mined for limestone.

The Dudley Trust's retrofitted 1930s working narrowboat was following us. It had to be electric because there are no ventilation shafts in the tunnel so a diesel engine could potentially be very dangerous. The driver was a retired policeman, a volunteer with the Trust. His knowledge of the tunnel surpassed its length and back again.

We learnt that the tunnel was built in sections. A shaft would be blasted out from above and workers lowered down to hew a suitable space out of the limestone. Each section was done by a different crew so the tunnel wobbles along: some crews made taller sections than others, and in a few places the limestone was considered hard enough not to need the support of bricks so, here and there, you come across wonderful caverns. Whole families, parents and their children, would work down below, boys from the age of nine and girls of twelve and up. In the cold and the pitch blackness, I couldn't help but think of those poor souls: I felt their presence all the way through the tunnel.

The first stretch glowed from the light outside, a sort of silvery green from the ivy, but very soon we had to turn on our head torches, which barely dented the view ahead. It felt utterly other-worldly as if we were travelling along the Styx. A quarter of a mile in, and the dark began to creep into my imagination. Half a mile in and the cold was seeping into our bones.

At regular intervals along the wall at head height, there are little holes where bricks are missing. This was the simplest way to build the tunnel. You would work till you reached head height, then build in a wooden support so that you could carry on up and build the arch. At the end, the supports were removed and the hollows filled themselves with all sorts of strangeness. Often there are large spiders hanging out. The tunnel is home to thirty or so different species of cave-dwelling spiders. If I shone my head torch around, I could see all shapes and sizes of spider dangling around us. Our boat guide, the driver of the working boat, told us they were all partial to biting anything they could get at. They hung like ornaments on a Christmas tree. There's not a great deal of food in the tunnel for hungry spiders – they seemed to be eating either each other or us if we touched the sides.

If the hollows didn't have any resident spider, they oozed limestone deposits. These were often white, but sometimes black, blue or sulphur yellow, depending on the minerals the water had picked up along the way. The oozing was most pronounced where there had once had been a shaft, the backfill making an easy passage for ground water. Often it looked like candle wax drip-ping out of the earth. It was hard and wet and rippled along the tunnel walls making a small space even tighter. Sometimes it formed in elaborate shapes, like boiled tripe. Those deposits glistened and dripped and crept into the tunnel, slowly but surely reclaiming the space, taking back the heart of the earth. On the ceiling there were hundreds of straw stalactites, thin limestone straws – water runs through the middle and rained minerals on us as we floated past. They are extremely fragile and easily broken. Each one gets to the ripe old age of twelve years and shatters.

At the halfway point, we took a celebratory rest, then slowly paddled on, mostly in silence. Dave had started to call out our progress as every hundred yards there was a mark to let us know how far we had left to go to the end. We were now both a little wet and cold so we decided to power on the last mile. A hundred yards later, a sign pronounced we were still only halfway. We joked nervously, and I wondered if this was some trick whereby we'd be floating in the middle for ever, like some sort of Purgatory. Or whether this really was the River Styx and the ferryman behind was following us so we couldn't return to the world above.

Dave told me that was typical tunnel fear: when he was alone, he said, and going down long tunnels on his narrowboat, he had a song he sang to remind him of the world outside. Slowly, in his rich tenor, he started to sing 'Summer Time', keeping the pace to his paddling, and I hummed along for a bit but left him to it. There was something deeply moving about that slow song in the dark, dank world. Eventually we hit a spot, a magical place, where we could make out the exit and still, if we craned our necks, see the entrance. The quirks of the builders meant it was gone moments later, but the sight of light was so gloriously welcoming that we paddled harder and harder.

As we came close to the outside world the light flitted about in a haze before us. Outside the tunnel, the canal was thick with a swarm of gnats of almost biblical proportions. An unappealing haze, but the only way out was through them. They were so new to the world, hatching around us, and so swept up in the fury of new life, that they didn't bother us, though I swallowed a few inadvertently. They hummed around, bounced into us, but mostly tried to follow us so that we arrived accompanied by thousands at the swing gate.

The warmth of the sun, the accomplishment of two hours'

paddling, the gnats, the bold young ducklings, the green haze of the park beyond, Dave's singing and a surprised gongoozler, who could hardly believe that two inflatable boats had appeared out of a hole where no one went, all added to the air of an extraordinary day.

We opted to take the narrowboat back. I sat at the prow by the headlamp, taking in the detail I hadn't been able to see under my dim head torch. Once we were out of the tunnel we took a quick tour around the limestone caverns. We had been underground for almost four hours and it was a relief to be back in the afternoon sun. We thanked the boat driver, said goodbye, and I took Dave back in my car to Alvechurch where he'd moored his boat for a little countryside air. That is one of the joys of being a houseboat owner: you can move home to a secluded towpath with cows for company or be back in the basin with the nightclubs and barflies. It suits Dave, that life, being able to change his setting whenever he cares to do so, and with such a network of canals to moor at in the Midlands, the idea is appealing. But I think I'd miss my garden too much.

*　　*　　*

I got home from dropping off Dave in his new rural idyll and fashioned some supper for H and me. The very last of the stored beets were a little too earthy in flavour, but there were fat bulbs of garlic to roast and lettuce from the garden. The last beetroot of one year and the first new lettuce of the next. I found a snail in my lettuce leaves as I washed them. For a while I watched it drowning in the washing-up bowl, then saw it emerge from its shell and, in shock, probe its watery world. And then I couldn't. I plucked it out of the water and put it into the climbing hydrangea by the back door. God knew what would happen to my garden if I went on like that.

For weeks I'd felt I'd been pulling away from the garden, ready to let it go for a freer life on the water, where I didn't have to tend anything, one in which I wasn't responsible for the order of things or how they flourished. Yet when I stood in my garden, wobbling about what it would mean not to garden, to want to be elsewhere, it was the only place to fall back to. That soft earth, worked by worms so that it cut like butter, the soft, dark soil that crumbled if pressured. Left alone to take the weight of the world, it still breathed. I stayed there pulling at weeds, cooing at seedlings, watering the tired and weary, protecting the young from the wind, cajoling the bent to stand straight. I stayed there until I had turned soft and quiet and capable of taking weight again.

9

I ploughed on down through the map of the canal network, heading out of town to suburbia, imagining a tunnel of green to get lost in. Instead I paddled past endless bland back gardens, some sweet, some individual, but most clipped and pruned, mown to within an inch of their lives or concreted over. Even the towpath side was a little boring, though the hawthorn blooms brought their heady, decaying scent over the water and left the hedgerows looking as if they were covered with snow.

I spoke to an old man who had been restoring a very pretty canal cottage. It had come with an acre of woodland and I felt a great pang of jealousy. Could I survive suburbia for an acre and a pretty gabled door? He wished me well on my trip and I paddled on down past more plastic fascia board and patio chairs. At one point I disturbed a mallard duck and her young. I'm ashamed to say that tiny ducklings are considerably faster swimmers than I am a paddler and I failed to outstrip their panic. The mother disappeared and I was left with five distraught babies that wailed and splintered off before regrouping and wailing again. Then, out of nowhere, the mother appeared over my head and landed in front of the boat. Imagining some sort of stand-off, I paddled to the side to see if they would regroup. The duck ignored her brood, allowing them to scatter again, then started to plough up the water. She raised her wings and, with great effort, zigzagged back and forth, creating giant ripples that I could feel under my boat. The energy required to make such a movement in the water is extraordinary. I started paddling again and she kept up the drama. She had left the ducklings far behind now, and they calmed down, perhaps in disbelief. I passed them, wondering whether she'd gone mad or was injured. I followed her doing that strange zigzag for half a mile or so until she suddenly decided she'd done enough and flew off to return to where she had come from.

The ploughing was just a ruse. The zigzagging disturbed the water perhaps so that I couldn't accurately see the tiny yellow heads bobbing about – or maybe I was supposed to think she was injured and thus an easy target, a bigger, tastier meal. The necessity of survival, the sacrifice and small acts of drama that are played out just to get by. I thought of my own dramas. Deep inside me I was unsettled, zigzagging back and forth, desperate to let something out, but I was still too afraid to admit even to myself what it was. So I just kept paddling.

The rest of suburbia bored me. At some point, I saw a big fish, close to the bank. It slipped under the surface, leaving a ripple of water that, again, I felt under the boat. I saw blue-tits, a fat magpie, several cats, some arrogant, others disdainful, four small dogs, an old man who suggested I had a pint with him at the pub, and that was about it. After two hours, I got out and cycled home. Training practice, I guess. I thought about the mother duck, her panic, her adrenalin, the wasted effort on the unknown, the bright-red boat. Perhaps I was scaring off all the wildlife on my journeys – I should have got a green one.

10

Dave persuaded me, although it didn't take much, to crew on the Birmingham Canal Network Challenge, a twenty-four-hour narrowboat race to cover the most miles across the network, whilst doing a treasure hunt of sorts. I thought it would be a good way to see as much of it as possible, to take note of where the best wildlife was and to get outside the city limits, which I knew I wouldn't manage by paddling alone. I also accepted because I was desperate for any sort of distraction, especially with endless locks and hard work, which would force me into a deep sleep, because I was unravelling inside. I was a cauldron of unease, bubbling up, ready to erupt. I couldn't stay still. I couldn't stay at home. I couldn't rest, and I couldn't talk to anyone about any of this because I had a great overwhelming fear that if I opened my mouth I might say how I actually felt. I might ask for what I actually wanted. I might start telling the truth.

I knew I had to do this. I'd started to see a counsellor to talk about it because I'd finally admitted to myself where it was coming from. At that point, though, I wasn't ready to let anyone else know, so I took on the Canal Network Challenge because the noise of the narrowboat engine would drown anything other than the most superficial conversation, the locks would exhaust my whirring brain and the walking between them might slow my thoughts.

There are a hundred or so navigable miles of the Birmingham Canal Network, but it's impossible to cover anywhere near that in a twenty-four-hour period. Most aim for around thirty miles, picking up extra clues on the treasure hunt, such as what the graffiti says on a certain bridge or the name of a nearby factory, as well as winning points for the size of your boat, the number of your crew and whether you can get to the finish line by two o'clock on Sunday. We had to take a six-hour rest period; we couldn't have extra people to help us at the locks, or change our crew halfway through. Some people took this race very seriously. Dave was one of them but, thankfully, Louise, his girlfriend, a little less so. It was agreed we'd make a half-decent attempt to gain a respectable amount of points, but we'd also stop at the pub and take a route that would allow me to see a little of the more unusual bits of the canal.

I told H that I would be away for the weekend on the boats. He took the news as he did much of my increasing absence, not with indifference but with a sort of stoical acceptance that my work, writing and lecturing, took me places and his took him to the pottery studio. We had always had an independent sort of relationship. He was the only person I could spend all day with and say very little to, deeply content that he was in his world and I in mine. I knew that he was lonely without me, that my absence meant more takeaways and junk food than I cared to think about, but I also knew he respected my independence. I went to the water a little anxious this time because each step away was no longer reinforcing our bond of marriage but reinforcing my sense of self, which, I was beginning to understand, was very different from what I'd thought it was. Giving up gardening every day, thinking about paddles and maps and places I'd never been to, even if they were on my doorstep, was establishing something new. If he sensed this, he said nothing.

*　　*　　*

On the day of the race, at 7.30 a.m., I met Dave and Louise on their boat for a hearty breakfast. We'd head off at eight to tackle the flight of thirteen locks out to Farmer's Bridge and the Jewellery Quarter, then to Aston. Dave had registered his boat and his start time. He gave me a brief technical talk on how to open and close a lock and, more importantly, how not to get your fingers chopped off.

I was feeling strong, ready to race, ready to run or cycle along the locks. My job was to close them so that Louise and Dave could race on to the next set. By the time Louise had opened the next lock and Dave had moved the boat into it, in theory I should be ready to start closing the gates behind him. We'd play tag all day.

Before the race, I had only opened one lock before and never closed one, but I had been devouring books about the women who worked in the Second World War on the Cut, bargee slang widely adopted by Brummies for the canal – the canals are literally cut out of the land around there, with steep, steep banks. Those women were the land girls of the water, keeping coal and goods floating up and down while the men were at war.

So, I knew something of the names of the parts and how much hard work it was going to be. We had forty-six locks to accomplish in eight hours. Our start point at Old Turn was popular – there were three boats ahead of us in the race, which meant breakfast at least could be leisurely. We had two boats behind us so I couldn't mess up the locks. There is an etiquette to how you should leave a gate for someone behind, plus there are anti-vandal locks to replace in cities because it is entirely possible, Dave told me, to drain a large part of the section if you open all the gates at once.

Old canals meander, like a river, working their way around difficult terrain, and often have few locks. With modern canals, those built from the mid-1800s onwards, no expense was spared in forging a direct route. Trade was driving business and, like a modern motorway compared to an old back road, little was allowed to get in its way. Modern canals tend to have high embankments to build the water above sloping terrain. If the topography was hilly you built a lock. If the land rose more steeply, you built a flight of locks, like a staircase, to move the heavy boats relatively effortlessly over a mountain, if need be.

A lock is a chamber in the canal with a gate at each end. The boat enters through one set of gates; these are closed, and the other set of gates is opened or closed to let water in, depending on the direction. The top mitre gates have a culvert at either side of the towpath that allows the water in or out. Often it glugs and splutters beneath your feet as you wind up the lock gear. The lock gear is a simple valve, traditionally a flat paddle, which you wind up manually with a metal tool called a windlass.

It works like this: you open the entrance gates and the boat moves in. You close the entrance gates and the valve is opened, which lowers the boat by draining water from the chamber. You then slowly open the exit gates and the boat moves out. If you are going upstream the process takes place in reverse – you wait for the lock to fill and lift the boat. Depending on the water level and the direction, the quickest you can get through a lock is about five minutes and the slowest can take ten to fifteen. If you meet a boat coming the other way through the lock, you're in luck: they will have set the locks in your favour, thereby saving you time.

A lock is a little like a bath with huge taps at both ends and a plug-hole at the lower end. When you open a lock, your job is not to leave the taps on with the bath unplugged because then the bath wouldn't fill.

I tucked the windlass into the back of my jeans so that I wouldn't lose it when I leant on the beam to open the gate. Dave smiled when he saw this and said, 'I approve of your traditional method of carrying the windlass.' He and I know that I'm made for this sort of work.

After a couple of locks I'd got into the swing of things, quite literally using my entire weight to haul open the gate. Forty-six locks later my body was exhausted. Every muscle had been employed to force water in one direction or the other.

There were numerous flights in that run, and as Louise and I began to tire, we started to slip up on detail. Take your hand off the windlass or, worse, remove it too early and the gate drops dramatically, thundering through the metal teeth, reminding you of how fragile your fingers are. Close a gate too quickly and it swings back open, forcing you to leap to the towpath to close the other side.

We encountered just two people who helped us with a lock, probably not strictly allowed, but as we didn't invite them to, I don't think we broke the rules. The first was another narrow-boater, moored up ahead, who had heard us coming. He readied the locks for our passage in time-honoured tradition. It's like putting on the kettle when you know a visitor nears.

The other was a young eastern European man sitting by the canal during a break from his work at the scrapyard. His English was limited, but he quickly grasped the task, took the windlass from me and rattled the sluice gate up fast, jumping the lock to help me balance the beam. We did the first gate in seconds and then he moved on to help me close the next. When I had to leave, I went to shake his hand and, confused, he bowed backwards from me. I grabbed his hand. His palm was so wide that I could barely get my hand round it. I felt the great power in his arms, but he was clearly embarrassed by his worn, filthy hands. We both stared at them, then I showed him my own grease-streaked versions and shrugged, grinning, while he grinned back. Just for that second we offered each other brief respite: he had taken the burden of the paddle and I, perhaps, had relieved his boredom. I ran off to catch up with the boat, turning briefly to see him watching me go.

*   *   *

The day proceeded, opening and closing, winding up and winding down. There was beer, music and some wonderful industrial views.

It was marvellous under Spaghetti Junction, the famous knot of motorways that swings over and around Birmingham, with strange pockets of wilderness and a bank of odd exotic blow-ins. Although narrowboat life is slow – the boats travel at three miles an hour – there was little time to think of anything other than gates and locks, locks and gates, which was all I had hoped for. For a day at least, I was consumed by gurgling, rushing water and I could think of nothing else. It was a wonderful release.

The following day was wet and cold. Dave had plotted a route that meant we met the majority of the locks on the first day. Without them, the day seemed to drag and my mind whirled. We wound our way back towards Wolverhampton via Channock Chase, travelling right to the end of the canal, where the great Chasewater Reservoir sits above. With few visitors, that basin was crystal clear and we watched fish dart among reeds and waterlilies. For the first time since the beginning of the adventure I could see the bottom of the canal. That spot was a pastoral idyll, with a small canal cottage, a lone moored narrowboat, coots and herons perching on the banks, idling in the nature reserve. Rabbits lolled slowly at the edges and in the early-morning light the grass glinted with dew. We journeyed back with the nature reserve to the left and a few lucky suburban houses overlooking the great expanse of green. It was odd to think that the centre of Wolverhampton was but a few miles away.

We travelled on into the nature reserve. There was a thin strip of woodland that no one could reach from the land, and there, in the dappled shade of those trees that pioneer such places, the grass had grown tall and thin. Unburdened by footsteps, this was virgin grass, each blade in a balancing act with life. Eventually they would flop over, rocked by the wind. But at that moment the grasses, backlit by the sun, each blade separate from the next as they eked out what little light the trees let through, were dancing to an ethereal tune.

As we chugged along, churning the water, we passed numerous

beautiful blue-brick bridges, like commas linking one misty vista to another. There were thick old oak trees, the sort you see in Constable paintings, and the muted hues of an ericaceous landscape, purples, reds and deep greens among patches of old grass. There were a few dog-walkers, but the slow, low drizzle kept the landscape unpeopled and, momentarily, I was lost in meditation at how breathtaking it all was.

Of course, bridges aren't placed to frame a pretty nature reserve. They were made for a reason and, despite its pastoral air, the nature reserve is burying old coalmines. The names of bridges give away the area's history: York's Foundry Bridge, Coopers Bridge, Jolly Collier Bridge, Coal Pool Bridge and Brick Kiln Bridge. Pit ponies, hurriers (women and often children who transported the coal out of the mine), other workers, coal, dust, hammers, pickaxes, shovels, tubs, coal corves (the small wagons pulled by the hurriers): those were what the bridges were built to carry. It's extraordinary to think that such an industrial past lies beneath all that beauty. Nature always moves back in, and if the rotting, tarred dark past of that valley can spring forth with such light and life, then the slimy, rubbish-strewn inner-city canals, with their tattered buddlejas and soot-leafed alders, can do the same.

We continued to chug along, the wind cold and the engine loud, with no locks. I chatted to Dave, gossiping about friends and life, and spent a lot of time staring at the water. The locks had kept my thoughts at bay. Without them I was like the white waterlilies that lined the side of the canal. When the boat passed them the wash, both on the surface and below, dragged the lily pads down and they waved as they sank only to reappear minutes later. I felt the sinking and reappearing fiercely.

*   *   *

Waterlilies are the trees of their world. They create woodlands and forest at the margins of their watery territory. Their large leaves out-compete smaller, more delicate marginal plants. There are canals where all that is left is a thin black line of water along which the narrowboats pass, while the rest is a thick bed of lilies, *Nymphaea lutea*, jostling for space. This waterlily is a beast: it has both submerged and floating leaves and muscles its way through any sort of water it cares to. The waterlilies we were passing were the white variety, *Nymphaea alba*, which has only floating leaves. Bright green and waxy above, deep purplish red below, the purple pigments are using the far end of the light spectrum. Green chlorophyll is of no use here: purple will concentrate what little sunlight hits that murky underworld into something useful. 'Purple is gay and bright whenever the rays of the sun are weak and shady,' wrote Aristotle.

The top surface shines because it has a thick waxy cuticle layer, which does two things: it keeps the leaves buoyant and the stomatas, the breathing pores, clear. On land plants, the stomatas are usually on the lower leaf surface. On land, keeping them open yet not losing too much water or respiring too quickly, is a considerable problem. The lower surface of the leaf is more protected, not in direct sunlight, and has its own microclimate. If conditions dry out, you will often see leaves, particularly those from tropical environments, roll themselves up to protect the stomatas. But the waterlily does not have that problem: it sits in a world with plenty of water. Its dilemma is how to keep the stomatas open without drowning the leaf. Hence it places them on the surface. Deeper within the leaf something else is keeping things afloat. Special spongy cells trap air, creating a huge amount of intercellular space. This leaf has its own internal lifejacket, forcing it to float upwards however many times it's submerged. Look at a cross-section of a waterlily leaf under a microscope: the upper and lower levels are packed with cells, as you might expect, but the middle is filled with balloons of air. Not drowning but waving.

Waterlilies do something else magical. Their rhizomes, horizontal roots, act as an oxygen line, dragging air to the tips of the roots, the rhizosphere, a microscopic world, a thin shield around the very edge of the very tip of the root. By passing oxygen down and out into the muddy, anaerobic world at the bottom of the canal, the waterlily is increasing the numbers of others that can live down there, aquatic insects, plants and amphibians. The benthic zone is the very bottom of a body of water, and the thin layer of soil and water that waterlily roots inhabit is known as the benthic boundary layer. Those that live there are the benthos community.

The word 'benthos' originated in the nineteenth century and was devised from the Greek word, meaning 'depth of the sea', by the German biologist Ernst Haeckel, who also came up with 'ecology'. He was one of Darwin's early supporters, a philosopher and wordsmith. He introduced the term 'world riddle' to describe the balance between the meaning of life and the nature of the universe. 'What is the nature of the physical universe and what is the nature of human thinking?' he wondered, in *The Riddle of the Universe* (*Die Welträtsel*). He believed that human behaviour could be explained within the laws of the physical universe.

The benthic zone is another of those edges where one world meets another. How everyone works together here shows how the overall ecosystem fares. The waterlilies blow through their root tips a fine layer of air that prevents everything down in that deep dark mud from suffocating.

The waterlilies also provide shade: sunlight concentrated through water is harsh for freshwater fish, which rarely have eyelids, or a shrimp small enough to fry. So, the waving lilies are the forests of this world, providing oxygen and dappled shade, shelter and homes to those that creep around there.

May arrived in all its lush green glory. My neglected garden sang despite itself, and the allotment sprang forth with free food when I bothered to visit. I felt a pang of guilt when I looked up from writing and decided that the day was good for paddling, not gardening, but it was only a pang.

Sarah and Ming were as keen as ever to explore yet more canals so I agreed to meet them under Spaghetti Junction. I took the train to Aston to do a mile or so on my own first. I passed a wharf, a scattering of back gardens, and a number of huge warehouses. Under a bridge just before Spaghetti Junction, I found a pair of men's black leather shoes and a crowbar. The shoes were ghostly, as if someone had just taken them off, the right foot standing on the heel of the left. I looked around hesitantly – I felt as if whoever had owned them was still present – and then I paddled like mad to get out of there.

Just as my heart stopped pounding, I spotted Sarah and Ming arguing about which side to paddle on. This was a regular event and every time it made me laugh.

We had a pattern now: they'd bring two cars and leave one at the end destination so we could all hop in, then pick up the other. They had left one car at Minworth, which wasn't where I'd imagined we'd go but they promised me there was a good pub nearby and we headed off, away from the roar of the motorways.

It was a long paddle to Minworth, five miles or so into the evening sun. It was a good one, though. We passed epic old factories, including the Cincinnati (they made machine tools), with its own bridge that goes to nowhere, and another abandoned space with a giant wheel that must once have propelled something but now stands alone covered with ivy twenty feet up, like some relic from a funfair.

We met various fishermen, who were after bream and carp. One tried to warn us that we'd get no further in our boats, and if we did, we'd be thwarted by tree roots and debris, which sounded like a good adventure but turned out to be lies. Where there had been dandelion and coltsfoot during the past month, there were now fat stands of yellow flag iris, majestic and brilliant among rotting lorries and ancient machinery. The far bank, where there was no towpath, was covered with May growth. Sedge tassels waved in the ripples as we paddled past, and alder roots curled far out into the water.

Numerous alders had been felled along our route. Their roots, like witches' fingers, stretched out to caress the water. The common alder, *Alnus glutinosa*, is native to Britain and Europe, Asia and North Africa. In short, it's got around. Grown wild, it is nearly always multi-stemmed. It has short rounded leaves with a cookie-cutter edge and, noticeably in spring and winter, round female catkins: dark, little fir-like cones that cover the ends of branch tips and persist well after they have released their seeds. It thrives in wet locations because it has a symbiotic relationship with a bacterium called *Frankia*. *Alnus* and *Frankia*'s marriage lets both soldier on where few others could. The bacteria fix nitrogen, allowing the tree to survive in poor-quality soil. In return, the bacteria are supplied with the sugars they need to survive. A mature tree will give up any spare nitrogen and phosphorus, which also accumulates around its roots, to others around it. It becomes a mother tree, supporting not only other trees but insects, lichen and fungi, which can survive only on the alder. It is also a pioneer species, breaking new ground, improving it and eventually dying out in the natural course of ecological succession.

You rarely find the alder in established woodlands because the young seedlings need light to germinate. It is a tree of the edges, of the forest, the river, the swamp, bog and canal. I marvelled at the ghost trees as we paddled along. I wondered if they would sprout again, or whether they would slowly rot away. Alder wood is soft. It once had great commercial value and was used where we'd substitute pine today. In Norfolk it was famed for clogs: an itinerant clog-maker would buy a tree standing, fell it, shoe a village and move on.

When we hit a series of locks, tiredness took over, and as I clambered out of the boat I lost my phone to the bottom of the canal. I watched it wobble down to a murky grave. It was always going to happen, at some point, that something would fall into a canal, but I felt clumsy. I wondered if the others could see how distracted I was. I wondered if they knew the thing I could barely admit to myself, that I was someone else inside, and that someone was at complete odds with my life.

Ming helped me drag my boat out of the water and the three of us carried the boats around the lock. I felt a bit like a child. I felt a bit lost.

Back in the water, we followed swifts chasing our prows to catch midges all the way to the pub, where we ended up among a sea of blue shirts watching Aston Villa lose. We retreated to the pub garden and watched a gang of feral children tear up and down the worn patch of grass.

I was edgy and restless. I laughed too loudly, drank too fast and licked the salt and vinegar from the crisps off my fingers too intensely. Again, I wondered if they noticed. Losing my phone felt significant: I was losing touch, losing a form of communication, letting go of a thread. Days later, I did just that. I unravelled my world. I shattered it and sat among the shards and fragments in shock.

11

What brought out those words? Why now did I have to admit to it?

A woman, yes, there is that.

Over time, such a long, long time, I had suppressed someone, a part of myself, so deep that there weren't enough words to make a rope and send it down to find her. But one day, standing on a metal bridge looking over a dock, she shouted so loudly, so suddenly, that I had to cling to the edge to steady myself. Sitting in a meeting later, I had to shout back silently to her that it was not in any way acceptable to turn my chair sideways and stare so hard at the woman beside me. But she forced me to stare at Charlotte anyhow, and I spent a whole meeting pretending I was fascinated by a light fixture on the wall behind, while the person I had suppressed deep inside me drank her fill.

She didn't want to be silenced, though, so I told her this: There isn't a rope long enough and there's a hard overhang – you're terrified of those – so you'll have to stay down there. There'll be time later on, I promise. I'll come and find you then. But she cared not for that promise, and without a rope and with no leader, she took on the overhangs and the sharp ledges. She became exhausted, lost weight. She became despondent but no amount of reason stopped her.

Then one day she, this other part of me, sat at the edge of our bed, turned to H and said, 'I'm gay.' Or maybe bisexual, somewhere in that grey middle. I was paddling out to a place that might be white or maybe it was blue-grey, like the gloaming before night, or pale grey, like the first light on a cloudy morning, but out I paddled.

That shattered him and she shattered me. But she was some warrior, that other me, and she only grew stronger in the following days. So I let her. Was it Charlotte who had brought out those words? The warrior shook her head and said pragmatically, 'She may steal your heart, she may be your one, but if she isn't I'll find you another.' And that was that for the warrior.

Of course, for me, that was not that. There were a thousand other questions, a thousand sobs, a thousand sad nights ahead, my husband fragile, fraught, wounded and mostly disbelieving. I ached to know whether I'd irrevocably damaged the most precious friendship of my life. I feared the answer. Nothing and everything had changed. I had to lose him in different ways now.

* * *

In the aftermath of coming out – such a strange term: it feels as if it should bring with it some form of celebration yet for me it was suffused in sadness – I moved out of our bedroom and slept in my study. Those first nights alone were washed in heartache and pain, saturated in loss.

And then I had to do something else: I had to admit out loud, outside our marriage, what I was doing and what I wanted. I wrote to Charlotte and told her that I had come out. I had convinced myself that I had walked up a mountain with her in Ireland so that I might persuade her I was worthy of friendship. I felt so out of my depth, I was quite sure that a woman like her wouldn't want a woman like me. I wasn't even a rookie – I was married. I wasn't thinking about the immediate present but about the future. I'd thought if the stars aligned, if I was very lucky, there might be a moment sometime in my future when I might be able to come out. I thought I could wait. I thought this for many reasons but, first, because H has an illness that would rob us of our future, his future. I had learnt to anticipate loss. I had never been able to think, we'll grow old together. I had always had to imagine a future where I'd be alone one day. And in that future I thought, naively, that perhaps, oh, please, gods everywhere, when that happened, it might just be that Charlotte would be there, single, and, oh, please, dear gods, I might just be someone she'd notice. In that way.

And she had noticed in that way. We wrote to each other. We flirted so cautiously, so chastely, lingering over a hug goodbye, me touching the back of her hair to feel its fresh cut, but she had made very clear that she was not going anywhere near. I agreed with that: I didn't want her to be second to anything. She had as much right to be loved wholly as H did, as I did.

And I wanted that for her, like I'd never wanted anything before, and I wanted it so badly for her that I wanted it beyond whether it was me or not. And I was still underestimating the warrior inside me: once you admit to yourself that you are a lesbian, you are that lesbian.

Although those days were filled with so much anxiety that I could taste it all day long in my mouth, I was also finding peace.

*　　*　　*

I might not have known myself as well as I thought. I might have spent every spare hour or minute and many that were not, trying to work out when I had missed the moment of recognising that I wanted to be with women, but I knew this much of my marriage and my principles: I was not going to have an affair. I was not going to test the waters first, take a dip, risk someone else's heart, my heart or H's heart to see if it suited me. I would tell H first. I would tell Charlotte. If the consequence of those actions was being alone in a bedsit six months later, that was my fate. I would be responsible for my actions. I would be transparent in my needs. I would not hide anything any more. I couldn't bear any more secrets. If it went wrong I would know at least that I hadn't lied to anyone, including myself.

I wrote an email to Charlotte, telling her I had come out to H and that she was the reason, but she wasn't responsible; I had no expectations, I required nothing from her, but hoped there might be a future for us.

*   *   *

I phoned my dearest friend and heard her quiet sobs as I told her the news. She queried and questioned and tried to reason. Perhaps in the end she believed that I had left one path for another, knowing there was no return. I sat on the bench in my garden, trying to hear her final words, and instead all I could hear were the carder, the buff-tailed and the long-tongued garden bees going to work on the raspberries. They sang their work song so loudly that I sobbed, 'Please shut up,' but they didn't. They didn't care for my world or my worries, just the shallow nectar cups, refilling and emptying before the petals started to unfold and finishing only when the last had fallen.

*   *   *

I went to Italy to teach for a week. Before I left I met Charlotte in a park in London. We sat under a spreading ruby beech tree with dry dusty earth that smelt of the day's heat. I can see the dappled shade of every leaf as it danced that evening. I can taste the earth, the wind, the sloe gin we drank. I can see the light pass through the glasses she'd brought for us to drink from, how she packed them away when it was time to go. I still feel my skin, the heat of my blushes. I can taste my desire and hers. There is not a single molecule that exists of me of that day yet my memory can bring back every sensation of those few hours under a beech because I was completely me for the first time. I was brand new and as old as the earth below me. I remember expecting to feel like a child or a teenager, and instead I felt entirely the opposite. I felt like a thirty-seven-year-old woman. I had never felt more like a woman in my life.

*　　*　　*

The Italian sun did me good. Cold dips in icy lakes renewed my energy, while plates of pasta and lake fish put meat back on my bones. I stood around late at night at the edge of the Quink-ink lake and watched fish leap and bats swerve. I peered into ancient dry-stone walls and picked out lizard skins, or poked fun at the funnel spiders by tickling their trap lines. I watched bees mine new homes and chased common blue butterflies. I took my hand lens to mosses and flower parts. I taught in a distracted way, but few seemed to notice. I counted the hours forward, then back to home and what lay there. Quietness mostly, little change, few words, just a slow saddened waltz as I picked apart my marriage to start a new life. I'd take any distraction I could and head out to the Cut at the first opportunity.

12

I told my family. I told friends. I told a stranger just to see how it felt. After a week of telling people that I had come out, I found it all deeply tiring. Most people were kind, a few unsurprised. My brother told me he'd been waiting twenty years for that conversation. A few people were shocked, a few made some unkind, unthinking remarks, but on the whole people were positive. I began to understand that there is no such thing as coming out: it's a daily negotiation. You are forever having to challenge the dominant heterosexual view. Ask anyone who is gay, even the most out-there, you'd-hardly-have-to-explain-it types, but they do. Ours is an increasingly open, fluid society, but it is still a very straight, very heterosexual world.

H told some people and I was utterly relieved that I didn't have to do it myself and, perhaps more so, that he had accepted it. I cannot say how he coped, but he did so stoically, humorously at times, with generosity at others. And people were generous about him too: they said kind, thoughtful things, which says a lot about the sort of man he is.

Talking about myself so much drove me to distraction, in part because it was one of the those funny shifts from straight to lesbian that you can't quite anticipate. As a straight woman, there were, of course, assumptions, but I didn't have to make explanations. As a gay woman, who passed as a straight, as in

I hadn't cut off my hair – 'Are you going to?' my mother asked, shortly after I told her I'd fallen in love with a woman – it wouldn't be simply the immediate period after I'd left my straight life that I had to explain: I will spend the rest of my life gently correcting pronouns and firmly saying, 'My girlfriend and I . . .' That you don't have to anticipate is one of the many invisible privileges of being straight. From now on I'd have to talk about myself to assert my identity. I found it tiring and a little too consuming so, once again, I found myself running to somewhere I could get lost.

*   *   *

I garden because I am. I belong to the garden rather than the other way round. I pour myself, sometimes quite physically, into nature because it is how I make sense of myself and my place in this world. The gardener in me observes, the scientist orders those observations into patterns, then the writer makes notes. The scientist shakes her head at these and cries, 'Dreamer,' while the gardener gets on with weeding. Once again, throwing myself into the detail of the world around me seemed to make most sense.

*   *   *

The bridges and tunnels of the canals are often dark, strange, sometimes lonely places. In the dark centre only spiders, other-worldly mineral deposits and slime mould exist, but at the edges, the edges I love so much in nature, I found something to fall for. Mosses suddenly spoke to me.

This was partly because I'd read the wonderful *Gathering Moss: A Natural and Cultural History of Mosses*, by Robin Wall Kimmerer. Kimmerer is a biologist, a moss expert, a forest lover, a mother and writer of Native American heritage. The book is a love story about her favourite subject, her family and its history.

In my time, I have sat through many lectures on the life cycle of mosses, ferns and lichens and never fully got it, yet after a few pages of that book I not only understood but could see. I took my hand lens to this new world and found a whole new crossing of boundaries.

In the tree of life, the bacterial soup comes first, then the *Archaea*, bacteria-like, single-celled microbes, and then, in all its glory, the *Eukarya*. This domain is packed with all that glitters and glows. From slime moulds to mushrooms, algae, liverworts, hornworts, mosses, ferns, horsetails, cycads, ginkgos, conifers, gnetophytes and, finally, flowering plants. And, of course, ourselves and our kingdom, Animalia.

Bryophytes – liverworts, hornworts and mosses – are the transition, if you like, between certain green algae and vascular plants. The stepping stone from water to land, and this is the bryophyte's major obstacle: how to avoid drying out? Many of this gang do so by living in moist environments, by rivers and streams, next to waterfalls, in damp woodlands and tropical forests. Others in the family live at the other extreme, in inhospitable deserts and on mountaintops. Mosses are one of the few plants that dominate large areas of the Arctic Circle and a few even contend with the severe cold of the Antarctic. Being next to a source of water is good, but bryophytes can live for long spells in barren places. They have a heady, possessive relationship with water, but when it's not there, they rest it out, waiting for better times ahead.

The other bryophyte issue is sex, which cannot happen if everything dries up. To prevent drying out, bryophytes have evolved to exploit the wonderfully soft and silent world of the boundary layer. And to live there you have to be small. It's their trump card.

Plants stand upright because they have a vascular structure, a xylem and phloem, a set of plumbing pipes that conduct water and keep them rigid. When the plant doesn't have enough water it topples, which is what happens when you forget to water your houseplant for a month. Bryophytes don't have plumbing pipes, so they can grow only so high. They also can't conduct water from the soil to their cells: their roots merely anchor them, which is why bryophytes just sit on the surface of things and are easy enough to pick off.

The tallest mosses are found growing in very damp conditions beside rivers, lakes and streams where the continually damp environment allows a little extra height, but even these are limited to the boundary layer, the very last space before you delve into the earth, where the atmosphere meets the ground. High in the sky, where birds soar and clouds race, is the fast-moving laminar flow. With no disturbance, air up there moves in a linear manner, with little or no resistance. Below that sits the slower, turbulent zone. This is where we live, though the layer reaches way above our heads. Characteristic of this layer, the air swirls and eddies as it moves around obstacles – build-ings, trees, mountains. This is the air in which doves tumble and leaves flutter to the ground. This is the space in which wind batters and tugs. It is the zone where air makes its mark on our world. It shapes and shifts, it prunes, flattens and grades our soil and the plants that grow on it. But just below this there is a very thin, fine layer, the boundary between air and rock, and here things move very slowly indeed. At the top of the boundary layer there is movement still, but as you pass down through it the air slows until it moves not at all. Air stands still because friction from the surface below stops it in its tracks. To the boundary layer in perspective, a moss is a giant in this world, a millimetre thick at most.

Think of lying down outside in the sun on a warm summer day. Your nose, your shoulders, your hips might feel a breeze, but the warmth that lulls you to sleep is in part the stillness of the air around you. Your back is firmly in the boundary layer. In the still, slow boundary layer mosses grow very well. Their shoots are adapted to slow down the air movement further and trap yet more moisture between them. They are intricately designed to keep water and warmth around them. In this tiny space, this scrap of an environment, bryophytes not only make a home, but thrive.

If you look at a happy, healthy moss you will often see long stalks, known as setae. They often tower above the protection of the boundary layer. Sometimes they look like golf clubs upside-down. The clubbed end contains the sporophytes, the reproductive spores necessary for sex. They thrust up past the boundary layer to release their fine spores into the turbulent zone, from which they drift off to find new homes.

The spores are like seed, the last element in the reproduction game. Bryophytes evolved out of a watery world in which eggs floated and sperm swam. To get around this, mosses developed something that all land plants would later adopt. They protected their eggs. Leaving an egg exposed to potentially drying out is too risky, so instead they buried theirs deep within the base of the female shoot, using the leaves around the base to cluster and keep them moist, creating tiny pools, which the sperm can swim into.

But first the sperm has to get there and it needs a continuous viaduct of water, whether from rain, dew or spray, along which it can travel. Again in this tiny world, the architecture of the leaves has evolved to create a miniature waterpark, a channel of water between leaves, using capillary action to move the sperm from one place to another, just like the canals and their boats move goods around the city.

Like any plants with a seemingly risky strategy for sex, scattering their genes to the wind or water, mosses produce a lot of sperm, thousands going in no particular direction as long as there is water to follow. Most get lost among the forest of moss leaves or hit dead ends and dry out. Just a few make it in their short lifespan to the egg sack. Here, if fertilisation occurs, the female shoot will nurture the fertilised eggs, using specialist cells in that leafy green shoot to feed the young. When ready the sporophytes' golden clubs will rise above the green mounds of leaves into that turbulent layer, well nourished and ready to spore to new ground.

I started noticing mosses everywhere. In part this was a survival strategy. I was back to looking at my feet, back to homing in on detail to block out the larger picture. I was also falling for mosses because there's only so many times you can note a buddleja or a cat's ear. The flora of my canals are limited. I found a lovely bank of cowslips. I've paddled past drifts of stitchwort and drunk in the heady scent of hawthorn and elder-flower over the dank smell of canal water. I've fallen hard for the palest pink bramble flowers and marvelled at dog roses tumbling down embankments, climbing over abandoned walls and through our junk, but it's hardly challenging. There is little I can't identify at twenty paces, and I was restless for a new subject. The miniature world of mosses was a perfect fit for their odd survival strategies in dearth periods, their instances on colonising new ground, the way they cling to the most unlikely places, but mostly because, once you take your hand lens and throw yourself into it, in Byron's words:

> There is a pleasure in the pathless woods,
> There is a rapture on the lonely shore,
> There is society where none intrudes,
> By the deep Sea, and music in its roar:
> I love not Man the less, but Nature more,
> From these our interviews, in which I steal
> From all I may be, or have been before,
> To mingle with the Universe, and feel
> What I can ne'er express, yet cannot all conceal.

The world that the moss inhabits is truly wild, somewhere to get lost, and the canals are full of this kind of wild. Mosses hang out under drip lines in bridges and tunnels. They run between the mortar lines at the edges of the towpath. They hunker down in the valleys of badly poured tarmac, cling to walls and cover factory roofs. They hang out round the back of trees, hiding in the gloom. They pour out of wastepipe outlets and make their way across abandoned hoardings. They are resplendent and impoverished, sometimes verdant, sometimes blackened, but they are always there.

13

H and I started to eat out a lot. Routine was painful when our house was no longer a home, and we were together but separate. The rules and boundaries were no longer negotiable: who should do the recycling or cook dinner was a little meaningless. Eating out was civil. It was a transaction, too, though. It encouraged polite behaviour. It was a little business-like.

Not long after I came out, when I was still insisting that we might find some strange solution to our situation, such as me living in a shed in the garden, in that period where I wanted to be let go but was still clinging, I noticed my husband was no longer wearing his wedding ring. I had moved mine from one hand to the other. I noticed the same mark on his hand as mine, the thin band of pale, shiny skin. I wondered if he, too, kept looking down at this absence, noticing it in odd moments. How light that finger felt, how bare.

Over dinner, he asked me if I'd sell the house. I told him I didn't want to and we tiptoed through the rest of the conversation. He wanted to live somewhere else: being in our house made him feel lonely and sad, while I was clearly growing happier each day. He said he wasn't angry. An hour later we sat on the sofa, watching TV. I laughed at his jokes. I realised then that such small acts of domesticity were numbered. They had always been numbered, but I started to count. I told him I wanted to be there for him still, to support him wherever his journey with cystic fibrosis was taking him, with future operations, and he nodded noncommittally. I felt myself clinging to that last act.

* * *

The house was quiet. The house was a mess. I learnt to live in a tiny bed next to my desk. I felt as if I had shrunk in that space. We agreed that I would buy him out of the house. Mortgage adjusters came and measured up our space, revalued our home. H bought new things for a new life, and our old life was lost behind cardboard boxes and particulars for flats. The dog sat between the two worlds and sometimes howled. My home shrank to a bike and a rucksack that homed either the boat or my belongings as I travelled between Birmingham and London to see Charlotte. And H, he came and went. I didn't ask where. I wasn't so much curious as grateful that he was independent. I had trapped myself behind his illness and had trapped him with it. Now he was free, autonomous, capable, singular, decisive. These things are how I might have described myself in our marriage, but I didn't feel them now about myself. I felt true, peaceful and in love. I felt myself, but I didn't feel decisive or singular or all that capable. I felt questioning.

Sitting in the boat one afternoon, as midsummer spread out across the water, idling away time before I had to return home to the mess and the single bed, I composed a long letter to Charlotte in a quiet basin that no one could reach unless they, too, owned a boat like mine. I stopped writing and noticed the reflection of the brick wall in the water. It shimmered and wobbled, refracted and yet was not so wholly different from its true self, crumbling from neglect. Usually the water is too murky, a sort of goose-shit green, and anything it mirrors is smoked with that tinge, but the sun had won out that time and the whole basin became a mirage of an Escher painting. You could almost run across it.

I watched the bricks and the fish, the carp, tench and pike, that rise for a lungful of air. Could they see those reflections? Did they know that above them towered walls of industry, or was this just another play of light on the edge of their world? I paddled over to the wall and ran my hand along the bricks. I wondered what the men, women and children who had shaped those bricks would make of their legacy, or of me floating around in a bright-red boat? Could they have imagined that this basin, part of the Typhoo tea empire, would be abandoned one day to sink into a watery decline? I wondered what it was like to be a pike in that murky world. Were canal pike shadier characters than their river cousins? Did they live more tenacious urban lives? Were they more street smart? I wondered about the bricks some more. Birmingham is its red bricks. They are everywhere, in factories, houses, libraries, sports halls, church halls, working men's clubs and art schools. When I first came to Birmingham my overriding impression was of a monotony of red bricks, of housing that ran in ribbons up grey tarmac. I thought everything looked the same.

* * *

Birmingham bricks are made from our thick vein of clay. This was formed during the Upper Triassic period, when Birmingham was semi-desert, covered with a vast, shallow lake that was below sea level. Here, layers upon layers of silt, salt and sand sediment began to settle. Such lakes disappear during droughts, leaving the sediment layers to compress with just a crust of white salt left behind. This is our bedrock, our foundation, Mercia mudstone. Travel to any of the affluent neighbourhoods in Birmingham and you see that it lines the front gardens and makes great lintels and footstones for the houses. On top of the mudstone lies an even thicker band of reddish-brown dolomitic clay, sometimes with green bands and thin sandstone bits known as skerries. Hit one and you've hit a brickworks.

You don't have to dig far to do this. The city is littered with old brickworks, mostly now turned into allotments. The bricks run from beautifully engineered examples to rough shoddy things that fall apart in your hands. Our red bricks define our city. The canals are often enclosed by towering walls of them that radiate heat in the afternoon and whistle the wind along on cooler days.

Birmingham farmers quickly realised that this difficult, claggy vein of clay, which is not easy to farm, could be made into money in the form of bricks and tiles for housing. The very same clay that made the bricks of my house. They sorted out Mercia mudstone veins where there was sand in enough volume to make bricks easily. The clay would be dug in summer and left to weather over the winter, where it would be either trodden by foot or ground in a mill by a horse, then hand moulded into bricks and tiles. The tiles were of higher value than bricks and were used mainly for roofing. They were vulnerable to the high temperature in the brick kilns, so were surrounded by bricks to absorb the heat. Those handmade bricks varied greatly in quality, but there was a considerable market for them, expanded by the introduction of the canals. Carrying tiles along rutted farm tracks on a cart is a quick way to damage your cargo. The slow, steady, smooth canal was a godsend. The slow, steady, smooth canal was also rather good for moving Welsh quarry slate, which flooded the market and so the tiles fell out of favour. The brick market, however, persisted and flourished.

The industrial revolution needed a lot of bricks and by the mid-1800s there were more than fifty brick-masters. Building land, particularly for terrace houses for workers, was often advertised with its assets of clay. Brick-makers spent the summers producing bricks and their winters brewing beer – we're a land of fine spring water too.

The red of our bricks indicates land-borne rather than seaborne deposits and erosions. It is red from iron locked in among the wet sand that oxidises on contact with air. The sand and red iron weren't formed in Birmingham: they were washed down by a great river that lay in the Mercian highlands. Those highlands included a great band of trees that were eventually compressed deep into the earth to become the coalfields that fuelled all the industry around here.

I ran my hand over the bricks and looked at the dust on my palms. Either side of where my wedding ring had sat the skin was white and paper-thin. The callus was no longer needed and, like a snake, I was shedding my skin, my past life. On my right hand there were blisters from where the ring was making its new mark. It hurt to paddle with the ring on the wrong finger, and in the end I took it off altogether. For an hour or so I belonged to nothing but the water. I was tethered to no more than the journey.

I finished the paddle with a tiny stretch that runs under Birmingham's answer to the High Line Park in New York, an abandoned viaduct high above the city filled with a forest of wildlings – birches and field maples, mainly. Except Birmingham's viaduct can't be accessed and thus it is just a beautiful bit of Victorian engineering with a fringe and flop of green hair.

* * *

The next day I picked up where I had left off. I'd seen the goods and loading bays of a disused factory, which would have allowed narrowboats to unload directly into the factory: that I wanted to explore. They tended to have some sort of awning, usually of corrugated iron, and might have several bays and a channel or two. This one was home to a family of geese. The gander honked loudly and the young scattered at the first sight of my boat. I decided to cross the channel to get out of the way but beached myself on a brick wall that wasn't apparent under the dark-green water. In my long YouTube trawl to understand my boat better, I had seen a film that showed you how to pass over shallow water. A flat-bottomed skegless boat is ideal for this. The paddler on YouTube suggested that you throw your legs over the inflated sides and lift your arse up so that you're behaving rather like an octopus that wants to hug the boat, thus relieving weight from the base – it's aptly known as 'doing an octopus'. I flung my legs over and lifted my arse. It worked a treat and I floated over the first bit of the wall and, feeling rather pleased with myself, used the paddle to push myself off the next bit. The paddle got stuck and my octopus position quickly became untenable. I ended up in front of a large gang of young men and a lock-keeper (or, at least, a man who wore a lock key around his neck, which is as good as, these days), throwing myself onto the submerged wall, my feet in the goose-shit-green water, to yank the paddle out. At that point I realised the boat was not inflated enough so I had to bend over in the water and use the emergency mouth pipe to fill it. A slow, laborious task that made me look even more ridiculous. In his thick Brummie accent, the lock-keeper kept asking if there were more of me to come, and in my present position I couldn't help but lose it. I fell into the boat in a fit of hysterical giggles. The world didn't need more of me. I paddled off, trying to pretend it was all just an average day's work.

I made my way slowly around the bend and up towards the Gun Barrel Proof House, which is now a museum but still runs as a working proof house. Proofing is a compulsory test that all new shotguns and small arms must undergo before they are sold to prove, 'so far as it is practicable, its safety in the hands of the user'. A proofed gun is marked with a small stamp that bears a picture of the Crown and various initials. It's one of those hidden Birmingham gems. We make great guns in Birmingham, and where there are great gunsmiths, there are even better pubs. The Gunmakers Arms is well worth a visit if your train is ever delayed.

To the side of the Proof House there is a disused basin backed on all three sides by old warehouses and wonderful brick walls. On a sunny day, it's a warm, quiet spot, perfect for lying back in a boat and contemplating life.

I watched condom packets and Carling Black Label cans float by as the sun danced through the toadflax, and the blackberries eked out a living in cracks in the wall. There was a large gang of geese and a handsome alder, the necessary buddleja scattered about the wasteland, and a heron or two. Lying in the boat lazily, I watched a huge pike swim past and saw carp rise for mouthfuls of air. Around the corner, men sat vainly waiting for a catch, while all and sundry flopped about in the filthy water. It was not pretty, but strangely comforting. In truth, I was exhausted by everything, the worrying, the thinking, the falling in love, the ecstasy, the joy and the heartbreak. Lying about in the boat, counting cat's ears and ragworts, was hidden bliss. I lost an hour to the sound of the fish, imagining their underworld, swimming between shopping trolleys and industrial waste, darting between sunbeams, wallowing in the boundary layer, a foot or so of waste, calling that rubbish home.

After a while, I decided I should leave. To get to that quiet basin I had had to pass under a bridge that had been blocked off by the council. Behind the fence, under the bridge, carefully hidden behind what looked like council-erected boarding, a home-less man lived. He was quite something, built like a steeplejack, all muscle and power, silent, only just acknowledging me when I asked permission to pass through his home. I wondered if he was some sort of canal-side prophet, like Boeotian, the first Bakis (Bakis was a name bestowed on Greek prophets between the 8th and 6th centuries BC), who lived in a cave.

His house was carefully constructed from others' waste and hidden so that only those who boated through could know he was there. There was an enclosed bedroom, a sitting area with a wood-burning pit, where it looked as if he fed the geese – there was a large tray of corn in a small kitchen area. I grew so fond of his home that I would visit periodically to see what additions he'd made. The walls were fashioned from hoardings, lined with plastic. His bedroom was often decorated, once rather elaborately with women's handbags. I've passed by to find him hammering, drilling and sawing. He'd always stare very hard at me as I paddled by and flicked a finger as if to gesture me through his bridge home. Once when I returned, he was washing his clothes, his shoes and finally himself, looking up casually as I paddled away. I thought about a gold handbag and the string of plastic pearls I'd seen hanging in his room as I turned the corner to an onslaught of geese mayhem.

The wannabe lock-keeper was idling on the paddle of the lock and shouted at the geese to move out of my way. The young took flight and I was left with the angry male, honking and posturing. I'd become quite used to this by now from ganders, but the lock-keeper feared for my safety and announced that he would walk 'George' out of my way. I paddled slowly with the odd pair, George bellyaching the whole time, the wannabe lock-keeper and I meandering along to the bridge, when George took flight and the lock-keeper stayed at the foot. I said my goodbyes and paddled off with speed back under the viaduct forest.

14

H has spent his life in and out of hospital. It is par for the course if you're living with cystic fibrosis. With the change, the worry, or just someone else's passing bug, he caught a lung infection in late July and had to go into hospital for a round of antibiotics. I visited as I had always done, naming the colours of the linoleum floors after wildflowers – poppy red, hawkbit yellow, cornflower blue – as I walked to the ward. A nurse I liked seemed totally shocked when I appeared, then looked at the floor, the wall, at anything but me. I attempted to negotiate this bug as I always had, asking about drugs and progress, but ultimately I was now just a visitor, with no right to sit on the bed or question the charts. We played Scrabble every day, and for the first time, H taught me how to be a more tactical player, or perhaps it was the first time I'd listened to him. His directions were softly spoken, as if he was saying, 'In your new life you might do better if you understood a few things.'

I was alone in the house, which I had previously always dreaded when H went into hospital, but now I found it quiet and peaceful. I embroidered in the sun-drenched kitchen, listening to the radio. I lingered over the bookshelves and read poetry. I made meals exactly as I liked them and raided the fridge for scratch suppers. I liked this quiet world. If that sounds selfish, it was. I was pleasing myself, putting myself first, and I questioned it endlessly:

what sort of person was I? One who was going to carry on, I guessed.

* * *

Sarah, Ming and I met outside the Fiddle and Bone pub in the centre of town. Sarah and Ming were already in their boat, paddling around, and in my haste to join them, I failed to blow mine up properly so for the whole journey I felt as if I was dragging a dying balloon through the water. We agreed to go up the Main Line towards Wolverhampton, finishing off what had been our first paddle together. This stretch is known as the Engine Branch and passes through Smethwick on the edge of the Black Country.

We passed the Icknield Loop and the Boatyard, which was now thick with green as ferns, nettles and toadflax clothed its banks. I waited a little bit longer, past Soho Loop, past luxuriant stands of yellow flag iris and water dock. Then I waited a little bit more, paddled further, and admitted everything.

I nervously blurted out my situation. 'I think I'm gay,' and then, 'I am gay and I've told H.' I added that we were separating, then paddled off to pretend to look at a plant. Sarah was having none of this, and they were by my side in a few strokes, laughing, teasing a little that I might have felt judged by them.

I told them how tortured I felt that it had taken me so long to get there, that I had had to do this to H. Why had I not realised earlier that I was gay? With great empathy, Sarah said, 'Surely the only answer to that is love. You didn't know because you loved him and you waited because you loved him and you're doing it now because you love him.'

She said she was relieved because they had both been worried about me. 'I knew you had something to say, that you were bursting, and I wouldn't have guessed, but it makes a lot of sense.'

Then she wanted to know if I was seeing anyone. I stared at

the water and shrugged. I wasn't quite ready to tell them about Charlotte, though I could tell they had guessed.

There is a good reason why everyone jokes that lesbians are best friends with their exes. They mostly are because at some point you will run into your ex. I didn't know Charlotte because of Ming and Sarah, I had arrived there separately, but now Sarah's ex from way back when was my present, and I was little reticent about what that meant.

We agreed to head on and paddled at a good pace so that we left Soho quickly behind and found a tunnel I had spotted and wanted to explore. It was blocked by a hanging piece of plywood that kept narrowboats out, but in our boats it was possible to squeeze under it. The basin was larger than I'd expected and backed by a dilapidated factory on one side, some waste-ground and part of the still-standing façade of an older factory on the other. The whole basin was heavily silted up and the margins thick with irises, flowering rush and water dock. It was sheltered and warm, and beckoned to be explored.

At the furthest end a tiny tunnel was just big enough for my boat, but not Ming and Sarah's. The water was only a few inches deep and I was forced into the octopus position to move forward. The front of my boat was weighed down by the bike, and as I tried to manoeuvre it forward something caught my eye in a factory window. The glass was broken and had been patched up with green plastic. Inside, the factory was dark and I assumed I was imagining things, but there it was again. A small hand waving and then the face of a young man with dark hair and eyes. He waved again – he looked as if he was standing on tiptoe. He pointed, gesturing to me to take the tiny tunnel. I was unnerved. Why was he in an abandoned warehouse and what did he want me to see? I pointed him out to Sarah and Ming and he waved at them too, then pointed again to the tunnel. We agreed that there was something unsettling about the scene. Although it was apparent he wasn't trapped, we felt uneasy. We decided to get out of the basin quickly, which wasn't easy because both boats were beached in the silt, but we worked ourselves out, paddles thick with industrial slime, then slid back under the blocked-off entrance. The hanging plywood swung precariously, a guillotine in the making.

On the other side, we continued to head out of the city and pass various strange things. Sarah picked up an orange, but decided against keeping it, then spotted a small green soft ball, and we saw numerous coconuts bobbing about. The coconuts became a bit of a theme and gave the journey something of an abandoned-carnival air. Ming spotted a lone goose egg on the ledge of a blocked-up tunnel, but on closer inspection it smelt foul. Accumulating random canal flotsam was becoming a habit and added to the joyously childlike air of our adventures. Our conversations might have veered all over the place, from life worries to casual observations, but the joy of those strange expeditions lay in how full of play they were.

The towpath was wide and green out there, full of ferns, hawthorn, roses, birches and pretty little veronicas. From the corner of my eye I saw something white flowering and instinctively turned back to see what it was. To my great delight, I realised it was watercress, a healthy stand of beautiful green leaves crowned with tiny white flowers, like snowflakes. Watercress doesn't need to grow in water, but it does need wet roots and thrives best in fresh running water. Deep beneath all those dense fern roots there must have been a spring. It was such a welcoming sight in an urban area to find something like that, not that I'd suggest anyone should eat it: this was no Hampshire chalk stream, but deep in the centre of industrial Birmingham, a stone's throw from Smethwick, it was a heartening sign. Coconuts and watercress, what unexpected finds. A big fat fish rose to the surface, as if to champion the cause and I floated around happy.

We'd come four miles or so and decided to head back to town for food. On the way we passed the Soho Loop and, buoyed by the evening sun, decided to finish off by paddling that way. It added another two miles to the journey so we stopped just before

Asylum Bridge and after the prison to snack on nuts that the girls had brought. This time round the loop seemed warm and friendly. We munched the nuts, hoping for a full bottle of beer to float by instead of empty cans.

We paddled along, exploring the margins and looking for new finds. The last half of the loop is often windy and the paddling got the better of me, so I hooked myself up to their canoe and they towed me for a bit. It was an odd rhythm, being dragged by their boat, facing backwards and using my paddle as a skeg to stop the boat swinging from side to side. It's strange to look at the canal backwards and I enjoyed the tug of the tow, the kindness of the two people prepared to drag me along to the next stage.

I cannot tell you now why it took me so long to tell them when they were such natural allies, but I guess I was a little embarrassed, perhaps about Charlotte but also about coming out late in life. The hardest people to come out to, however close you are to them, are other gay people. You long to be accepted, but you feel too old to be seeking approval.

* * *

We ended the trip in the pub, discussing everything from the menopause to the need for a different kind of club night in Birmingham. We discussed our various options on where to continue the evening but ended up uninspired, and they agreed to drive me home.

On the way back to the car Sarah pointed at our version of the High Line Park. 'Can't you do something with that?' she asked. Just a few days earlier I'd been trying to persuade my friend Lucy that the abandoned viaduct was a perfect project for the National Trust. Now, in a fit of enthusiasm, we decided to break onto it. Sarah doesn't drink, but Ming and I were merry with beer, so the setting sun and the lack of a good venue meant that trespassing was suddenly a brilliant idea. Before I knew it we were rolling under a metal gate and Sarah was tackling a twelve-foot-high spiked fence. An extraordinarily good climber, she did this with grace and ease. Rather strangely, I'd decided to go paddling in dress shoes so I was on the top of the fence, negotiating the spikes under her guidance, but in completely the wrong footwear. It was easier than I'd expected.

Ming, however, got stuck. Sarah placed her palms over the spikes so Ming didn't impale herself, then didn't make a sound when Ming leant all her weight on them, a gesture of love if I ever saw one. But she was still stuck, and ended up in a fit of giggles, which infected us all. Here we were, three grown women, hanging off a metal fence for anyone on the railway line to see. This was not the point to get ourselves noticed, so Sarah and I hunted for material to devise a way down. I found a pallet and we both found some strong orange straps. We tied the straps into a loop that we could hang over the spikes to make footholds for Ming to lower herself to the pallet. A lot of giggling later and we got Ming down, even though she suggested we leave her on top of the fence and continue without her. We hid the straps and the pallet behind a buddleja for the return journey.

The first stretch was an overflow car park for a wedding venue. There were lovely bits of flora on that waste-ground. In the late evening sun the pale yellow-green flowers of a stand of mignonette, *Reseda lutea*, fluttered. It's a wild flower of disturbed calciferous soils, which this urban rubble wasn't a million miles away from. Young buddlejas and handsome brambles, with beautiful blush-pink flowers, were dotted in the concrete cracks, and a huge pile of rubble was almost high enough for us to clamber over the next metal fence.

We stood precariously on the rubble and took in the view. There were another two metal fences before we'd be on the viaduct, but up there, with a glowing pink sunset, it looked marvellous. A great mile-long curve of dense green trees and the city, with its comical skyline of Selfridges bubbles and the Rotunda cones beyond. Our city, beautiful Birmingham: we swelled with pride, and the playful nature of the evening meant that just because the rubble pile wasn't big enough we wouldn't be easily put off. Ming decided to manhandle up it an abandoned sofa full of strange Sharpie-pen drawings of old men's faces. Her giggles got the better of us. Although it was quite clear that the sofa wouldn't help, we grabbed an end each and wedged it up against the fence. The sofa was rotten and I was the only one small enough to bridge it so I could stand on top of the fence and take in the next bit. Even if I was brave enough to leap down, it was clear we would get no further: we'd have to come back with machetes. The brambles were years old and a deep thicket of them reminded me of Richard Brautigan's 'Blackberry Motorist', a prose poem about taking on epic wild blackberry patches and going deep into their hidden caves to hide:

> There were so many blackberries back in there that it was hard to believe. They were huge like black diamonds but it took a lot of medieval blackberry engineering, chopping entrances and laying bridges, to be successful like the siege of a castle.
> 'The castle has fallen!'
> Sometimes when I got bored with picking blackberries I used to look into the deep shadowy dungeon-like places way down in the vines. You could see things that you couldn't make out down there and shapes that seemed to change like phantoms.

That was what I was peering into, a strange playground of torture that my dress shoes and thin trousers were no good for. Ming documented our progress with some fine silhouette pictures and declared the climb worthwhile, then realised we might be spotted by passing trains as we headed back. Emboldened by our progress, I took the final metal fence too fast and ended up hovering just above a spike, my feet dangling. I panicked, I couldn't hold my weight, but just as I felt the spike prick under my arm, I was steadied. Sarah, one arm clasping the fence, was holding me up with the other and guiding me to a better position. Later, when I examined the cut in the mirror at home, I thought of the extraordinary strength she wears so lightly.

15

The next week, Ming and Sarah were away and other friends were out of town. Everyone was elsewhere. I was a free agent and took myself off to the canals to finish a journey I'd started with Ming and Sarah, up to Winson Green, a few weeks earlier.

I had the use of the car. I didn't drive much, which made me nervous behind the wheel, but suddenly I was able to embrace the freedom. I could get quickly to all the off-the-motorway stretches of canal. I wound down the windows and turned up the stereo, like a teenager.

Seeing the city from its motorways added another layer to my map. Once you get used to reading the canal topography, you know exactly when you're above or beside one, even if it isn't obviously visible. I no longer had to consult the map to find them – it was like sensing the sea before you can see it. I had a canal sixth sense. I could tell from the landscape, the change of buildings, the type of bricks or blank spaces that the canal left, however deep it was buried below. You can read the canals in the horizon, once you know how.

I drove to Winson Green and parked on one of those typical Birmingham streets, the sort you see in the TV show *Peaky Blinders*. Little red-brick terraces with front doors that open from the street straight into the front room. Summer had bathed the somewhat tired street in pretty light, but it was treeless and backed straight onto a busy main road. The only green space was at the end of the terrace, a small triangle of overgrown council grass and a weedy sycamore. The courtyard gardens were mostly filled with rubbish and old beds. That street spoke of the hard, obdurate world of inner-city living.

This section is along the main drag to Wolverhampton. Within a couple of miles it splits, and there is an older, meandering canal with various locks and side lines, and a straighter fast route built in the early nineteenth century that takes the boats into the Black Country. This is the dark, dirty, beating heart of the Midlands and to this day it belches acrid smoke, while the metal and steel factories boom, if not exactly to the march of late capitalism. This is old industry hanging on, for what it's worth.

I took a set of bridge steps down to the towpath and decided to walk a mile or so before paddling. I'd done that stretch on the water and had spotted a few wild spaces on the sides that I wanted to explore, plus I wanted to find the watercress again. I was curious to see whether it was growing in spring water or something less desirable.

I met two fishermen, no one else. The day was warm and I felt it stretching out, relaxing its muscles. The banks were steep there and covered with a mixture of pioneer species – birch, alder and brambles. Layers of sandstone were exposed here and there, and the soil was wearing her acid colours: cinquefoil, sorrel, hawkweed and bracken ran along the top of the bank and tumbled over the sandstone blocks. I found a bramble whose flowers showed a strange fasciation: the chromosomes had doubled up and tripled up again, and there was nothing but a mass of stamens. It was a grotesque-looking thing so I stopped to photograph it. Most fasciation results from mechanical damage when the shoot is young and the cells undifferentiated. Often fasciation looks like someone has squashed the stem or flower with a hammer. Fasciations are distorted and flattened. It's very common in asparagus, where it's known colloquially as 'beaver tail'. These are just oddities and nothing more. The rest of the plant did not exhibit anything out of the ordinary. I wondered if the fruit would be a mass of exploding cells, with hugely fat blackberries.

I wandered on as meadow brown butterflies flitted about. I longed to see clouds of butterflies, but they are largely a figment of my past. We have lost something like 40 per cent of our large butterflies and moths in the last sixty or so years. A few dominant species prevail. It is possible to find skippers, commas, peacocks, orange tips and admirals. I know where to look for common blues, and a few brimstones visited my garden early in the year. I grow enough cabbages always to have large and small whites fluttering around the garden, yet there are so few in general that even these are a welcome sight. Often I allow them to shred at least one or two brassicas because I'm soft, and desperate to see the spread of their wings as they bask in the sun.

The ancient Greeks named butterflies after the Greek goddess of the soul, Psyche, because they believed that these fragile, seemingly floating things were a living embodiment of our immortal souls. Psyche was married to Eros, the god of love, or if you were Roman, Cupid, the god of desire. But their tale of how they got there charts the complications of bringing the soul and love together.

There's a copy of Antonio Canova's wonderful sculpture *Psyche Revived by Cupid's Kiss* in the Villa Carlotta at Lake Como. During a complicated visit to the Underworld, as one of many tasks she must fulfil to win Cupid, Psyche takes the lid off a jar she should have left alone. She was told to bring back with her to the world a jar of divine beauty, but the one she has selected contains everlasting sleep, deeper and darker than the River Styx. Thus she is trapped for ever in the Underworld – until Cupid draws the sleep from her face, pricks her with an arrow and carries her back to the world above. Cupid has wings because lovers are flighty and likely to change their minds. He is boyish because love is irrational.

There are two originals, one in the Louvre, in Paris, the other in the Hermitage, St Petersburg, and many copies, like the one

I was transfixed by when I visited in June, teaching the gardens of the lakes. I often feel conflicted by marble sculptures, particularly those of the Renaissance. It was, I think, the beginning of the end for us. When we could take resolute, unchanging stone and turn it into flesh, to depict nature better than it is in reality, we elevated ourselves away from our world. It's not technology – cars, planes, rockets or computers – that will be our downfall, but art. When Canova chiselled and polished Cupid's wings so that, backlit by the afternoon sun, they become almost transparent, golden, like the wings of a brimstone butterfly, that was when we lost our way. When art imitates nature, when marble becomes flesh, we are seduced away from the true nature of the material world, in which death is present for everything. I fear that many of us believe we will find another fix for our environmental mess. But the ninth mass extinction is here on your treeless street, on a towpath without clouds of butterflies, and it is on the windscreen of your car, from which you haven't had to clean splattered bugs for years.

That sculpture of Cupid locked in a kiss to wake Psyche after her visit to the Underworld is one of the most erotic things you can look at in the cool of an Italian villa. Well, it is if the woman you've fallen in love with looks much like a boy.

I followed the meadow browns as they danced onto the water mint that had come into flower. Further along there was a patch of coarse mint and I imagined the sort of supper you could forage from that strange world: a carp or bream that had absorbed heavy metals from the mud on the canal bottom, some watercress growing in spring water surrounded by beer cans, and mint tea from the questionable soils of the towpath, a feast of things filtering out our waste.

I tripped past a bank of fireweed or rosebay willowherb and nodding foxgloves, the final fingers of flowers at the top of the bending stems waving me on, and eventually I passed the bridge where we'd last got out and blew up the boat for a paddle.

The first stretch of the journey was a little dull. The towpath stretched out and the far side was walled with brick factories. I came across a signpost: I could go right back down the Soho Loop or continue up to the Smethwick Junction locks. There, I could either take the Main Line to Wolverhampton, which is eleven miles or so, or bear right up to the Spon Lane Lock. I continued straight on to Smethwick.

I passed a lovely little iron bridge that would once have led to a factory. Blocked off, silted up and full of reed sweet-grass and branched bur-reed, and where this grew thick enough, plant debris had accumulated for the fireweed to establish itself and was blooming merrily away. I love these waterside gardens, so pretty and delightful. There is nothing rare about them: these are the common inhabitants of polluted or nutrient-rich waters, able to withstand whatever is thrown at them. They garden themselves so well.

A little further up I passed a beautiful chimneystack and an abandoned factory. The factory courtyard was full of dumped rubbish and old bits of machinery, twisted rusting iron and steel limbs, broken windows, with pulleys hanging like lost eyelashes. It begged to be explored, but not perhaps alone.

Next door a factory was being pulled down. A crane smashed, a digger manoeuvred the spoil, great billowing clouds of red-brick dust sporadically engulfed the canal and I had to wait, paddling in a circle until it settled. There was a strong, acrid smell of melting plastic and paint stripper. I passed a giant metal water-cooler, blue paint peeling, and beside it, a strange series of shallow tunnels under a bridge that must once have stored something, but now housed mummified pigeons.

In the light of all this, the wayside waterweeds were quite something to thrive here. The water was thick with some sort of slime that coated the paddle. When I got home I had to scrub the boat, the sticky slime having left an unpleasant watermark.

By Smethwick Lock's first gate there was a corner thick with bulrushes and yellow flag irises, of which the inflated seed pods were so swollen and heavy that the flower stalk bounced and nodded as the ripple of my boat passed it. I decided to explore the next lock because it would give a view of how many more there were to come. I had failed to bring a map and I'd begun to find locks tiring. I didn't want to spend the rest of journey hauling myself in and out from lack of foresight.

Two young ducklings panicked at my arrival so I hung back to wait for them to get out of the way. There was a small bridge before the bottom lock: one side was clearly very old and then it had been extended, probably to take cars, at a later date. The older half was decrepit, the mortar falling out, much to the joy of the funnel spiders, which had covered the arch in new colonies, a white, crocheted blanket of traps. I teased a few trap lines and saw spidery legs poise to pounce.

At the top of the lock I could look down a bank to the Main Line canal that runs parallel with the old line. A beautiful little tollhouse, used in the nineteenth century to collect fees from passing narrowboats with cargo, was sadly burnt out, and a modern housing development, at complete odds with all the industry around it, sat to the side of the old line. The canal was thick with waterlilies and plantain, and in the middle I saw the strangest thing. A pretty little roving bridge, with fancy brick-work, and beyond it more canal. A canal that was floating above another canal, the Main Line, which sat below. It was Engine Arm Aqueduct, and had fancy ironwork, the detail painted blue and red, the rest slick black. Some bleach bottles were floating down the middle of the water and it was barely wide enough for a narrowboat. My paddle was too long and hit the sides so I had to use it as you would in a canoe, single strokes until I'd reached the other side. A bright-red boat on a floating canal with bleach bottles bobbing along, faded to the same blue on the ironwork. It was hard not to feel pleased with the order of things, floating about in mid-air.

On the other side of the bridge canal, there were old factories, some disused, others not. An old man sat on a beaten-up office chair, staring at the water. I waved to him and he looked quizzically at me, but seemed to decide at the last minute not to say anything. I paddled on around a corner where I could see the Main Line canal below, so that strange sensation of floating on air lingered. A wall of a beautiful great factory was slowly crumbling into the water. It was covered with buddleja and had a large chimneystack. Its arched windows would have suited a church, one dedicated to the gods of commerce, perhaps. In any other city it would have been redeveloped into fancy apartments, but here it homed only weeds and a large fat dragonfly, which hovered alongside me, eyeing me up. I'd found a crumbling paradise. I snapped a few pictures, pleased with my little float and all the wild things around it.

I noticed a female mallard duck behaving very oddly. Ducks, I'd found, were very wary, more so than any other wildlife, of the red boat. She ducked her head so very low into the water that her whole body was submerged, head and neck stretched out so you could barely make out her profile. She snaked through the water.

It was such a strange sight that I moored up to watch her. She hid under some overhanging buddleja and I couldn't see her, until she startled out, exposing her plucked body. She was moulting. Mallards mostly moult post brood-rearing. They need new flight feathers for winter, which requires energy and usually takes place while the weather is still warm and there's plenty of food about. But it's a risky period, especially for the females. Without feathers you can't fly away from predators. On top of that you may succumb to nutrient deficiencies and stress. My duck's odd behaviour, hiding her bare body under the water, was a tactic in disappearing. I was supposed not to notice her. I was breaking a cardinal rule of nature-watching: I was peering too long into the private life of another being, staring too hard, disturbing the natural order. I felt uneasy suddenly and paddled away, followed by the large red dragonfly. It flew up close and stared. Nature eyeballing me now. Are you moulting too? What's your private life like? I tried to busy myself with peering into gaps in the crumbling wall, then paddled up to the gates of the private moorings at Engine Basin and peered into that too.

I decided to stop bothering wildlife and turned back, meeting my plucked duck again on the way. I took one last look at the fine factories and headed back across the aqueduct. On the other side, I slid with the boat down the embankment and relaunched into the ramrod-straight Main Line canal. The banks were covered with fireweed, campanulas, foxgloves, achillea, and wall lettuce, which ran through a ribbon of summer-blond grass. All the time there was an electrical buzz of crickets. I watched some hawkbit jiggle gently in the wind, and the canal lapped along the edges as the breeze picked up. Along a modern factory wall ivy climbed, like an army scaling a castle. I passed an abandoned toll island, now flattened and entirely taken over by bryophytes, mostly dry as dust and resting till the next rain.

Along the towpath clover flowered gallantly, despite the industrial waste in which it grew, and was visited by a lone fat carder bee. Despite the oil-slicked water a little fish leapt ahead of me and the sun broke from the clouds. Amid the pollution it was still possible to detect the smell of a forgotten August when, in childhood, summer stretched out and everything bleached itself in the slanting light. That scent of dry earth and ripening brambles, the way your skin smells when slightly sunburnt, the taste in the air of fruition . . . and then the panic that it will be another year before summer opens her doors to let you out again to play.

16

I am terrified. I am the woman who left her sick husband. I am the one who failed on 'in sickness and in health'. I am gossip. I am selfish. I am.

I did it not only to survive but to thrive in life. I chose to do it. Women are born to be guilty, to be guileless, to be selfless, to give. I see it flicker in people's eyes. 'I'd not do that.' I see it flash through their responses. I have to steady myself for that, and what I cannot hear, what is said behind closed doors, what is whispered down corridors or along phone lines.

I chose to do this.

Everything in this new light has to be re-examined. I am carrying a huge, unwieldy backpack full of things I will need for my future. Each item I add to that burden must be carefully examined, evaluated – 'Will this be of use?' If it weighs more than its value it has to go. I stand among these littered emotions. I pick my way out and don't look back. My refuge is plants.

* * *

I started to stare at blackberries. Growing out of canal-side buildings, growing out of towpath edges, over bridges, by the waysides. Of course they are ubiquitous, but with little else to look at I took them on. I stared hard, drank them in.

There was much more variation than I'd expected. Some flowers were a pale carmine, flushed with excitement. Others were white, some antiqued, more with just a hint or dusting of pink. The leaves differed in size and hairiness. Blackberries come from the rose family. I don't think I love a family more for its kin, its genus. They are all my favourite sorts; apples, plums, raspberries, apricots, pears, dewberries, tayberries, haws, quinces, medlars, cherries, damsons, nectarines, peaches, loquats, strawberries and, of course, roses. It is a family to sup: 'Stay me with flagons, comfort me with apples; for I am sick of love,' as the Song of Songs goes.

There's nothing quite like the right blackberry, those big fat berries that are twice the size of normal ones and juicy-ripe. As you pick them you're stained with their blood – you eat as many as you pick. Like Brautigan, you get greedy and make inroads into the bush to get at those that are just out of reach. In my park you can chart the blackberry progress by the new roads, the kids bravest enough to learn how to throw themselves on top of the brambles and flatten them without too much damage to clothing or skin.

Blackberries, *Rubus fruticosus*, are not a single species but an aggregate. There are four hundred or so microspecies, subtly different in leaf, flower, shoot and fruit. The fruit is not strictly a berry but is composed of drupelets, each fleshy outer part surrounding the seed. Together the drupelets make an aggregate fruit.

Some of that fruit is polyploidy – it has double or even treble the chromosome number in the fruit so the berries are twice the normal size. A normal fruit has diploid chromosome, 50:50 from each parent; polyploids can still have equal parts from both parents but sometimes they are unevenly distributed and the result is weird-looking berries. On top of that, like the dandelion, blackberries are rather fond of apomixis, a sort of gender-fluid position for the plant in which it adopts neither sexual nor asexual reproduction. The term comes from a mixture of Greek words, meaning 'away from and mixing'.

Asexual reproduction in blackberries tends to take place when those arching cane tips hit the ground and root, eventually creating a new plant, slowly gathering ground. Sexual reproduction depends on bees: those large pale flowers are bee heaven and the Rosaceae family has a long history of seducing the bumbles and their friends.

Apomixis is most often associated with polyploidy so those extra-fat juicy berries are going it alone. In apomixis, the plant produces fruit and seed without fertilisation. The plant forgoes sex, but still ends up with its product, the seed. However, in apomixis the seed is genetically identical to the parent. Every dandelion you will ever meet is exactly the same genetically as every other dandelion. They are clones marching across the world in unison. Brambles often do the same thing.

It's a response to a good environment. Why bother with bees if you can be self-sufficient? If the environment is right, the plants will romp away by themselves; if the environment changes and genetic diversity is advantageous, the plant will revert to the old way. Apomixis is a sure way to pass on certain genetic traits – there's no gamble. If you've got good genes, why mess with them? Dandelions, brambles, hawkweeds, certain grasses take this route because they are successful plants, weedy, ubiquitous. They can survive in all sorts of habitats and there's no need for them to mess with sex to keep going, so they don't.

As I floated past great blackberry plants dripping out of walls or scrambling over embankments, I thought of all the far edges where there was no towpath and no other pickers. I started to get excited about the canal bramble jellies I might produce. Brambles are known to pull pollutants from the soil into their system. They are not deep-rooted, but neither was the soil around there and it would carry some trace of its industrial past. However, I knew a few corners where little had been disturbed and I intended to float under certain thickets and pick my fair share.

When I think of those fluid brambles or bryophytes that don't mind changing their sexuality, if necessary, when I think of worms that are hermaphrodites until the right one comes along, or follow happily companioned drakes that don't notice a passing female, I wonder why we've made it all so complicated for ourselves. At the end of the day we are a species, not even an aggregate one, just a single species.

17

As summer progressed, I split my time between London and Birmingham. I loved being in London with Charlotte, but I also felt lost, out of place. I'd done new-to-London before, but my past London had vanished and now I was exploring a city that was familiar but so very different.

Charlotte and I cycled along Regent's Canal up through Bethnal Green and onto the Hertford Union Canal. John Nash, its engineer, began work on it at the start of the nineteenth century, and it meanders across the city until it meets the much more regimented Hertford Union. The canal seemed wider than much of the Birmingham Canal Network, but perhaps this was a trick of the eye – I was looking down at it rather than paddling in the water. It was also harder to read. Every inch of this is recently developed land, so there's no sense of history to tell us why the canal is there, other than fleeting examples of old factories, though many of these are set back from the towpath or canal edge and are most likely twentieth-century additions. By 1948, as with much of the network, this canal's commercial use was dwindling as rail took over. The buildings aren't there for the businesses to use the canal: they are there because the canal-side land was cheap – no one wanted it.

London's canals have a clear monetary value that Birmingham's have yet to acquire. Home-owners like to have a balcony overlooking water or a garden backing onto it. This canal's towpath has many users too: parents with push-chairs, dog-walkers, cyclists, skateboarders all jostle for space on it. There are far fewer fishermen and those there are seem young and hip in comparison to the ones I see at home. Tempers frayed every now and then, and the towpath had none of the sedateness of Birmingham's pace.

We stopped at a bar, ordered pizza and drank beer. We sat on a scrappy bit of concrete embankment and I dangled my feet just above the water. We discussed life, slowly layering our under-standing of each other, peeling back bits and covering areas we weren't allowing each other to look into yet. I toyed with a water dock and counted the wayside weeds. Some hipster kids had pizza delivered to their blow-up dinghy, which was tied to the side, and someone threw pebbles at them from a bridge above. I know that all these people are good for the canal: their footfall means that the towpath is bike-friendly and smooth, that the wildlife and water quality are monitored, but it was a little too populated for me. I was almost glad when we were back on the roads. I realised I wasn't yet ready to share my canals with too many others.

*   *   *

Back in Birmingham, I met Sarah and Ming at the top Perry Barr lock, outside the keeper's cottage. We hadn't seen each other in weeks and it felt good to be back on the water together. We took the Tame Valley Canal, which runs almost parallel with the River Tame, until we could turn off down the Rushall Junction, the southern limits of the Rushall Canal, built to bridge the Birmingham Canal Network and the Wyrley and Essington Canal.

Both canals were built in the 1840s and are ramrod straight. The Tame Valley Canal cuts through 200-million-year-old sand-stone and the sides soar above your head with beautiful beeches and rocky outcrops. The high embankments meant that the paddle was sheltered and warm. At the edges of the canal, hart's tongue and ladder ferns grew thick and luxurious in the shade, and brooklime, *Veronica beccabunga*, grew where the dappled sun fell. We passed under the truly magnificent Freeth Bridge, which is now just for pedestrians to use, a wonderful towering industrial relic. It was built in 1848 and named after John Freeth, a canal engineer and clerk to Birmingham Canal Navigation. Sadly, he was not the same John Freeth, an innkeeper and poet, who wrote a number of popular songs in the eighteenth century about the Birmingham canals that a friend had urged me to download for lonely paddles when I needed a little motivation. My favourite is a sort of pub song about the price of coal, called 'Birmingham Lads':

> This day for our new navigation
> We banish all cares and vexation;
> The sight of the barges each honest heart glads
> And the merriest of mortals are Birmingham lads.
> Birmingham lads, jovial blades,
> And the merriest of mortals are Birmingham lads.

Which could have been sung about us on that paddle: we were so carefree with our evening ahead.

We passed through thick patches of floating hornwort, and the margins were lined with arrowheads about to flower. The water felt clean on my hands, the wind was gentle and we paddled hard for an hour or so, catching up on news between strokes. At some point we found a dead cat, a huge dead pike bent in half and a young dead magpie. I prodded the pike, commiserated with the magpie and didn't care to look closely at the cat. Dead things on the Cut are a given, these days. You start to understand why it has been referred to as Dead Dog's Ditch.

The canal eventually pulled out of the sandstone dingle and rose above the city so that all you could see from the water was sky and the fringe of towpath weeds. In the water, there were swathes of white and yellow waterlilies, as well as more arrowheads, patches of floating hornwort, and lesser spearwort, a waterside buttercup. It was the richest canal I'd seen for plant life.

As the canal is high up and thus exposed, it was difficult paddling if the wind whipped up. To stop and admire a plant for even a few seconds meant being blown several metres backwards, so we pushed on.

In a smallish clump of white waterlily we found a decapitated doll's head and Sarah rescued it for Ming, who wanted to put it on the front of the boat. Out of the water, the doll's red hair entangled with hornwort seemed somewhat Medusa-esque. Other than dead animals, the other canal guarantee is old plastic toys. Cycling along the towpath to meet the girls, I was spooked by a large plastic horse floating just below the water's surface. That, and coconuts: we saw yet more mysterious coconuts bobbing about.

Several bridges later we were out of the wind but into the roar of the motorway. As we cornered the bend we turned left to head towards Rushall Junction. Ming found a water snail, a sure sign that this was the cleanest water we had yet paddled. But it turned out to be dead. A concerned jogger, warming up against a bridge, clearly caught only the latter part of our conversation and called to us, asking if we needed help. A little confused, we waved at him. We were still such an odd sight on the canals – we'd yet to meet any other paddlers and often elicited strange responses from passers-by.

Pleased that our journey was now halfway through, I produced two bottles of beer, which I'd been keeping cool, from the bow of my boat, and Sarah brought out chocolate and orangeade. This, I fear, didn't help our image much with the jogger, who looked even more baffled by us now. We paddled on, balancing the drinks between our knees, and met a friendly gang fishing, a family having a picnic at one spot and a surly young man at another who refused to look up at us.

On the Wyrley and Essington Canal there were many soft edges and, despite the noise of the motorway, it was so picturesque. There were great banks of flowering rush, one of our prettiest waterside natives, with its blush-pink cupped flowers on tall stems, and behind that a row of fireweed, which towered above the water, then ran off into a thicket of birch and hawthorn. More arrowheads, a fringe of yellow waterlily as far as the eye could see and, on the other side, bulrushes, yellow flag iris, a great stand of reed sweet-grass and branched bur-reed, with its funny yellow pom-poms just coming into flower, and a smattering of water plantain. We slowed down to enjoy the scenery and the girls quizzed me gently about where I'd been in the last few weeks. There wasn't much point in hiding Charlotte – we all knew where I'd been – and any coyness on my part was faintly ridiculous. I remember telling them that Charlotte's house was very clean, which seems a strange detail now. But, then, it *had* seemed very clean and ordered in compar-ison to my cluttered, unsettled one. I remembered feeling that it was very masculine, all dark walls and polished wood, everything so carefully ordered. I sometimes felt frivolous in that designed space – I was like a wildflower meadow beside a mani-cured lawn.

In later months I took to caring for Charlotte's houseplants, nurturing the neglected Chain of Hearts back to life. I started to squirrel in more plants. Finding them watered, added to and cared for in my absence was the surest sign of love.

Sarah said I seemed happy and relaxed. 'I am,' I shouted, from a bank of flowering rush. 'I am!' And then we talked about how manic I'd been, how they had worried about me. How, when it came down to it, I had had no choice. I either stayed silent, broke down or, worse, took everyone tumbling with me into depression. I had chosen the only route I'd felt I could: I'd spoken up.

The thing you hear over and over again when you come out is how brave you are. It doesn't feel brave. It feels far from that. You don't feel like you're winning anything. There is little valour in coming out late – you confuse people: they feel they don't know you any more. You feel the same thing about yourself. You spend hours wondering whether there might have been a better moment. Ultimately it becomes, if not now, then when?

I don't think coming out brings happiness. I know it can result in a lot of sadness. It isn't a guarantee of anything other than perhaps not letting yourself down. What coming out brought me, though, was a peace I hadn't known you could possess. A strange landscape inside which you can wander, not to lose yourself but to explore. My stampeding beast, the one inside me that had raged, had come to a standstill and was now watching everything with new wonder. I stopped and stared at life now, not because I yearned to be lost in the detail but because I wanted to sup it all up.

There were moments when my landscape shifted, wobbled, was uncertain and sometimes terrifying. The first time I met Charlotte's friends: a tableful of perfectly polished haircuts is all I can distinctly remember – that, and my wild hair, scraped knee from hauling a bike about town, and how very childlike and nervous I felt.

There were those who thought I should and could have waited, those who thought it had been a choice. I hesitated and stumbled over how to refer to my husband (until a kind listener gently offered up 'former partner'), telling my boss, and meeting my first disgusted stare as a stranger realised I was kissing a woman in public. These things, the etiquette, the language, the pronouns, the glances and glares, the thrills and disappointments and, oh, the opinions, don't add up to happiness, but they don't detract either. I finally understood what Philip Larkin had meant when he wrote, in 'Born Yesterday':

> In fact, may you be dull –
> If that is what a skilled,
> Vigilant, flexible,
> Unemphasised, enthralled
> Catching of happiness is called.

Because happiness is just that, caught for a bit. But peace, to be able to hold that inside yourself, well, that's worth singing about to all the opening blooms of the waterside. It's worth a steady stroke of the paddle. It's worth peering over the side of the boat to get lost in the water weed. It's worth it all.

The three of us floated down the canal that evening, drinking beer or orangeade, examining flowers, until we met a man walking along the towpath. We'd passed under the M6 and were in some quiet suburban part of Birmingham. He said hello, so Ming and Sarah did their usual and charmed him into conversation. He turned out to be full of canal lore and, for a while, I floated behind them catching the words as they drifted. It turned out he was giving directions for the next chapter of the journey and all the best real-ale stops along the way. Then he talked about a couple of old friends, who used to come once a year to the lock we were just about to happen on and sit in a motor boat in the lock with a case of beer, drinking and going up and down as they endlessly opened the lock and closed it again. 'Don't know why they did it, but they did it every year. Must have been some anniversary. There's a lot of anniversaries on the canal,' he said. And then he explained the coconuts: every year a woman came to the bridge and dropped one, with a marked calendar and a bunch of flowers. Her young son had fallen off the bridge and drowned in the canal. It was, he said, some Asian tradition to do with death rites. Then he wished us well and walked on.

We had seen so many coconuts – too many to represent lives, surely.

When I got home I googled coconuts as religious offerings. It's a Hindu tradition. The coconut is thought to represent a human head, with its rough hair, like ours, the hard shell, like our skull, the coconut water, like our blood, and the white kernel, our soul. To break open a coconut is to break with our ego. Coconuts play a part in *daanam*, they are ritual gifts given as part of the thirteen days of mourning, fishermen throw them into the sea to appease it, and they are dropped into rivers as an offering to honour birth, death and, it seems, almost everything in between. The coconut is offered to Mother Ganga, goddess of the Ganges, or Apam Napat, god of cosmic waters, to show respect and ensure blessings in this life and the next. The offering is not complete unless it is put into the water. Saris, flags, flowers and ashes are offered to the water for safe passage from this life to the next.

We had paddled through a thick slick of grey film on the last paddle just as we left the sandstone embankments. I had wondered aloud whether it was some sort of pollen, but perhaps it was ashes. As there is no sacred river in the UK, the Hindu community had taken to the canals. The Cut has become a substitute Ganges. I would have thought that there were no gods for man-made canals, no spirits or muses that would want to claim the industrial age, no water deities to worship at unholy springs, but now that I was there floating around, finding myself, I could see there was a spirituality to the place.

18

August was a glorious month, often hot with that lovely low slanting light that picks out emerging seed heads and burnishes everything golden and orange. My office at home basked in late-afternoon light that filtered through the stained-glass window H had hung to hide the hideous plastic windows the house had come with.

I had been sleeping in there for months now, in a tiny single bed. Slowly the floor space was disappearing as day and night began to blur into each other. There were embroidery projects that I churned out to keep my hands busy, and too many half-finished books I turned to at three a.m. for distraction. Night creams and lip balms littered the spare space on the shelves, and the dog took up the better part of the bed. That little boxed world was wearing thin.

Outside the room, I had Sellotaped a 1960s Ordnance Survey map of Birmingham to the wall. I had been colouring in my progress along the canals. Thick green strokes to show where I had gone, greasy lines where I had run my fingers over routes I would take. It was a romantic gesture, really, as large areas on the map no longer existed, buried under modern development, cleared as slums or hidden under motorways. Rotton Park is now Edgbaston, St Bartholomew is now Digbeth, and I realised as I consulted the map that the bit of the Cut I'd been so excited about doing in early September was now a housing estate, a shopping centre and waste-ground. Disappointed, I decided to do a familiar stretch from Bournville to King's Norton in hope of spotting the kingfishers that were supposed to be nesting there.

I blew up the boat by Bournville station to the sounds of train announcements. 'Do not ride your bike on the platform,' said a sign, because, I thought, you may just misjudge the whole thing and end up in the canal. I listened to the names of places I might visit if I stepped off the towpath. Would I rather spend the day in Ludlow or Malvern? I tied the bike to the front of the boat and dropped down into the water. I immediately met a disgruntled fisherman and gingerly paddled around his very long line.

I pottered along the margins and peered into potential kingfisher nesting sites. You can usually smell a kingfisher nest before you see one: the rank stench of rotting fish pervades the air. I couldn't smell anything other than canal water and paddled on.

After a while I felt distinctly bored by that stretch. A few more things were in flower since my last visit. There was some amphibious bistort I hadn't spotted before, and water mint, banks of it. Fireweed flowered, reed sweet-grass waved as I paddled past, and I found a good patch of water plantain, but as I wanted to see kingfishers, the ubiquitous water plants, delightful as they were, were a little lost on me.

It occurred to me that I could call someone to chat with while I was paddling along, which might be a rather nice thing to do on a Thursday morning. So I called my mother.

She was unfazed by the noise of my paddle strokes or that random passers-by were shouting hello. We had a slightly stilted conversation about how little money I was making, which didn't add much to the *joie de vivre* of the journey so I returned to our common language of flowers. We have always been able to talk about flowers for hours.

We discussed the wayside blooms I could see and I tried to describe a plant in the Lamiaceae family I couldn't identify. She told me about some lady's bedstraw she'd found in the bottom meadow and how she'd staked it so that she could return next year to see it. She talked about the burnet saxifrage, *Pimpinella saxifraga*, that had come into flower in the top meadow and, slowly but surely, she mapped out her world in flowers. I was walking with her through the fields, poking at familiar wild things at our feet, discussing the merits of stuff that most people trample over.

She asked me about home, about H. We talked about divorce and hospital visits. I paddled on and turned left towards Stratford. I passed a magnificent oak and paddled into a tunnel of trees, the banks soaring up above. There were ashes, alders, oaks and beeches, some clearly still there from when the canals were first built. Trees that had watched the canal's commerce come and go.

We talked about why there were so few people, mostly men, on the towpath. I think the Cut is still viewed a little suspiciously by many. Some stretches, like the one I was on, are lined so deeply with trees, no visible sign of human habitation other than litter, that they feel remote, even though city life hovers just above the embankment. In the countryside walking and meeting no one is highly desirable, but in the city you question why few people are around. I realised that down on the Cut I shed my city ways, the cynic dissolved, and I became the kid who had grown up in the countryside. I said hello to everyone I met and happily stopped to pass the time of day. I was free and easy with my story, as others were with theirs. 'I like it down here,' I told my mother. 'It's like being home.'

She asked me about Charlotte, which she hadn't really before, though I had told her some. Unfettered by the journey, I started to talk. I told her of the things I loved, the surprises and delights of my new relationship. We talked about loss, about when and how my mother was orphaned, of when and how Charlotte was orphaned. My grandmother had died in childbirth having my mother and her twin. They never knew who their biological father was and lived with their adoptive family. It was a strange and often unhappy childhood.

My mother told me of my grandmother's second marriage. I was surprised by this: ours is a family tree rooted in oral tradition yet I didn't think I'd ever heard that branch of the story. She clearly adored the 'very handsome older man' who brought ease, perhaps, to her conflicted relationship with her mother.

She talked of how when her mother had had cancer, she and her twin, Dorothy, had nursed her to the end. This story is typical in my mother's life. From childhood onwards she had nursed things, tiny penny chicks from the pet shop, her mother, a hospital ward, great-aunts no one wanted, sick children and, finally, her dying twin.

Dorothy and she went to Southampton to tend their mother in her last days while Mack, her stepfather, and his friend, 'two subsistence farmers really', sat watching the cricket and feeding Dorothy's twins, as if they were motherless lambs that needed care.

I was so absorbed in this tale that, before I knew it, I'd arrived at the Brandwood Tunnel. I hunted around for my head torch so that at least I could see where I was going this time but found I had no batteries. Then, to my luck, a narrowboat appeared with two old men, one at the front with a camera ready to document the tunnel and the other steering from behind. They were clearly a seasoned crew. I shouted hello, waving my useless head torch, and they agreed to let me follow them through the tunnel. I hurriedly told my mother I'd call her back when I reached the other side and paddled after them.

Either I was getting much fitter or the pull of the narrowboat made paddling very easy. Mostly I had to concentrate on not going too fast and hitting the rudder. This was an old boat with gentle head- and rear-lights, and once in the tunnel, I could make out the captain, with his hand on the tiller. I felt the turbulence under the boat when I got too close, but I couldn't see a great deal of it. The tunnel, however, was bathed in a chiaroscuro glow and looked glorious as it revealed itself. When I'd paddled through it the first time, I'd come in from the other side and was too terrified to take in much of the detail but, dragged along by the narrowboat, I could study it. There were large limestone deposits, much like those along the Dudley Canal, in a tripe formation, dripping down the walls. But great stretches glowed with a muted Parma violet pearlescence. This was so strange and beautiful that I lost concentration and bashed the side, causing the captain to turn round. I waved, but realised he probably couldn't see me.

We passed the 100-metre sign, then the 161 marker, and the violet hue began to turn green. I remembered the green glow from my first visit. At the time I had wondered if it was some sort of bacterial fluorescence. Now I could see that the verdant outside was creeping in: we were near the entrance.

I thanked the captain and hollered to the man at the front, waving as I moored up to call my mother back.

I must have looked faintly ridiculous, paddling in my strange blow-up boat, talking to myself, but I liked the space my journey had given to our conversation. We had talked for so long that we'd moved on from casual chat into a proper conversation, the sort in which you wander wherever the terrain takes you.

She asked some more about Charlotte. And we talked about this being both a beginning and a continuum. She said, 'You're being honest to yourself and to others, but that honesty has the danger of newness to it. Don't lose what you built up before. You don't need to start again.'

Our talk felt timely. I had been keenly aware that I was stepping gingerly over a line that I wasn't sure how to define. That I was leaving behind my heterosexual life in many ways, but I wasn't sure where I was going. Or, to put it another way, I wasn't sure how far I would get from that wobbly line. I felt too queer for my straight world and too straight for a queer one.

The night before, I had sat upstairs in a bike shop watching an independent film about a deaf cyclist who had pedalled to the Arctic Circle. I overheard a conversation behind me in which a woman declared that 'It turned out I was seeing the most heterosexual of gay women possible. Our gender politics were all wrong.' A mild panic arose in me: could that be said about me?

My mother's gentle words reminded me of how I had felt during the film about the deaf cyclist. Some of us are always outside. I may remain outside both worlds. I may never quite fit anywhere, but then, as my mother's final words suggested, perhaps I never have.

'Bring her down when you're ready. Remember, we're a family who are good with extraordinary people.'

19

By late August I had settled into a routine of sorts. I spent my weekends in London and my weekdays working and writing in Birmingham. I had been out for just under three months, such a short time, really, but I had shifted my interior landscape irrevocably. I had gone from whispering, 'I am a lesbian,' to myself to saying it out loud. H had his own life, his own ways, and I had mine. It was strange to be observing this in each other, when we had been so familiar with our settled routine. There were few arguments. Mostly we passed like indifferent housemates. Occasionally he'd bring home new people, and I felt as if my private space had been violated, but I didn't feel I could claim that. The canal remained my escape, and when I was centred enough to find calm there, it was glorious. Seared into my memory are hot afternoons, the sun bouncing off the water, nature just being nature, and me being there to witness it all.

I took the train out to Aston. From the platform at University station I could see the canal on the other side. The train followed it, like a ribbon, through the city. The railway companies had been smart: they didn't try to forge out into the canal landscape, just co-occupied it. On trains across the city, the canal peeked in and out from its tunnel of trees. Straining to see it from a train window has become habit. I traced journeys I'd made and saw glimpses of adventures yet to come.

University is one of those lovely stations where the platform curves round so that your train will drive straight into the green. The embankments are so high and deep that a thicket of industrial woodland shrouds the railway, bathing it all summer long in a verdant glow. If you look at a satellite map of Birmingham between the Cut and the railway you can trace endless green lines hatched across the city, straight late-industrial-period canals and the curving, idiosyncratic ones of earlier attempts. On my own map hanging outside my office, my green ink traced them, and as the picture began to emerge, I could follow not only my physical progress but that of my emotions. It was a geographical map and one of my heart.

The sun shone and I was impatient to get onto the water and let the beat of the paddle centre me. At Aston, I hopped across the road, dodging some giant haulage trucks, and cycled along to the next lock. Star City loomed in the background, but the towpath was a pastoral idyll of blackberries and bracken. There was a good wind so the boat blew up fast. I lowered it onto the water and paddled off. It was not long before I was turning the corner to Spaghetti Junction. First there was a toll island, covered with bladder campion, dead nettles, golden rod, lupins, thistles in full bloom, stunted mallows and greater celandine. Toll islands are small brick islands found at various points on the network where a fee would have been collected as boats carrying cargo passed from one canal company to the other. They would have had little huts and buildings on them, but now they are just flat islands full of wonderful weeds. Herb Robert clung to its margins. It was rather lovely, and although the wind was picking up and the motorway roared, I felt calm descend on me. My paddling was steady and fast.

I turned to follow the motorway, and the flyover blocked out all natural light, except for one drainage channel that shed a beam on one of the giant buttresses that supported it. Here someone had graffitied a mild protest against capitalism. It was beautifully lit in its window of light, but the noise was too unpleasant to linger. On the other side there was a perfect no man's land. There was no towpath and it was surrounded by the suspended motorway, a true pathless wood where no one could wander. An island of birch and ferns that was astonishingly pretty and calm, despite all the traffic above it. The light fell in beams to add to its otherworldliness. I was half tempted to moor up, lie in those beams and explore that tiny untouched world, but I was also aware that few, perhaps no one, had trampled across that spot so it should be left alone. We go everywhere. We touch everything.

I sat in the boat, floating among rubbish, and pondered that strange space. I thought of the American poet Marianne Moore's wonderful line that 'the cure for loneliness is solitude'.

Happy in the thought and the view, I was disrupted by a phone call, which my poor modern habits dictated I take. I talked work with a friend while paddling along. I could see there were lovely things to look at by the motorway, but the roar of traffic meant I couldn't hear the other person properly. Before I knew it, I had allowed myself to float away from that strange moment of peace. I drifted down the canal, on my phone till I met a fisherman, who became annoyed by my presence and asked when I was going to move on. I ranted at him and my colleague. Suddenly I was bothered by everything. I said my goodbyes to my colleague and hung up. I dragged out the boat and glared at the fisherman for his frankly stupid tale about vibrations annoying the fish. I wanted to go back and argue with him about his quasi-science and his pointless sport. I wanted to point out that the big fish he threw back often ended up dead, curled up like they'd been tossed into a frying pan. I have inspected every dead fish I've found and an unhealed hook injury was often to blame. Mostly I wanted to shout at him for being in my space, and he wanted to shout at me for exactly the same reason.

Instead, I dragged the boat up the side of the lock, which was grassy, and pulled on my waterproof as it had started to rain. I sat by the boat, ate the cake I had brought for lunch, then hunkered down to wait for the rain to pass, sending evil looks and silent curses to the fisherman.

Beside me grew a feral cabbage. It looked rather resplendent among the grass and totally out of place. I munched more cake, then got back onto the water, slightly calmer. I floated over a wonderful patch of white waterlily and great mats of underwater hornwort. This stretch was clearly rarely visited by narrowboats and the water weeds were making the most of their freedom. Water plantain, arrowhead, bur-reed and flowering rush littered the margins while the white waterlily conquered the middle. It made paddling hard work, but among the hornwort I saw tiny fish dart in their playground. It was lovely, but suddenly I wanted to cry.

I called Charlotte. I knew why I wanted to cry but I was so surprised by those feelings that I couldn't trust them. I was in love and suddenly optimistic about my future. I spread it out and could imagine it basking in that optimism and its potential. I cried because I was happy. I also cried because it had become my default position. It was easy to cry, these days.

I wept down the phone, proper sobs where I lost my breath and gasped for air. Love and support bubbled back to me. I cried so hard that I let the boat float into a thicket of brambles that wrapped their thorny selves in my hair while the thickest, juiciest blackberries burst on me and the boat. I continued to sob and she continued to say steady things until I was quiet and tired, my face hot. We said our goodbyes, me apologetic for yet another outpouring of emotion.

Eventually I untangled myself and paddled on, down an idyllic little strip, with no idea where I was going. I started to see apples bobbing in the water, hard green ones with a bright-red flush. At first, I wondered whether they had been thrown in, but there were far too many for that. There was also a huge dead carp, its orange underbelly bared to the world, and later a medium-sized pike. I prodded the fish and wondered who would end up eating them. Would they be devoured by other fish or eventually sink to the mud below? I swerved between banks of waterlilies and floating islands of hornwort, watching the little fish dart, flicking out offending bits of rubbish as I went.

A young couple with a baby marched past, he furiously in front, she with the pram rushing to keep up. At one point he was left with the baby and she went up the side of a bridge. Minutes later she ran back and they both marched on determinedly. I wondered idly what they were up to. I met them later with the rest of their family. They were coarse fishing, the baby asleep in the pram. The young woman had gone for more bait in a fishing shop located in an old factory beside the canal. A whole family fishing and a baby lulled to sleep by the lapping of the canal.

I felt as if I'd paddled into a new country. I had little idea where I was on the map. I'd taken a turning without much thought of where it went and now I was exhausted from all the tears. Exhausted by the realisation that, for the first time in such a long, long while, I'd start to look at my future and not fear it.

I was coming to the end of the run: there were locks ahead and I didn't feel like scrambling in and out. I was tired and wanted something other than cake to eat. As I eyed up the best side to get out from – I always favoured a grassy bank, however covered it was with goose shit, because it was kinder to the boat as I dragged it along with the bike on the front – I saw a flash. A brilliant blue-green that turned like a fighter jet on its side to expose its orange underbelly and came to rest on an overhanging branch at the other side of the canal. I held my breath and carefully slowed the boat. I knew that the kingfisher had spotted me and would take off again soon. I waited and watched.

And then, just like that, another flick of iridescent blue and emerald, a dart to the water, a splash and it had gone.

There were two. I very slowly moored the boat and watched them flick from one side of the canal to the other, then up into a row of poplars.

A few years ago, in the depth of winter, I discovered that a kingfisher was visiting the pond I passed daily on my way to the allotment. I would hold my breath as I turned the corner and climbed the steps, praying it would be there. More often than not, it was. The pond is heavily silted up and there are tiny sticklebacks, as well as newts, which make good winter hunting, I guess.

The kingfisher was never around in summer, when the River Rea was probably better fishing, but on stark grey winter days I might see it. I started to view that flash of blue-green as a sign. A visit would mean a passing or a shift in things. I didn't expect to see the kingfisher often, but when I did I took the bird to be my talisman, as if it was telling me, 'Be ready.' I loved that bird. With time and patience, I spotted the pink smear of lipstick on its beak: it was a female, a queen-fisher. When one winter she failed to appear, I mourned her passing and keenly felt her absence each time I wandered past the pond.

The rational science-minded version of me scoffed while the romantic melted a little at the sight of two kingfishers. I felt loved, and my one lone bird had become two.

* * *

Kingfisher blue: an electric flash of cobalt that dazzles down its back of emerald green. The tail feathers appear blue and the back feathers cyan. It's a trick: those feathers are colourless, until they're hit by a wavelength of light. They are layers of transparent material arranged so that they are not quite perfectly aligned and thus, as the bird darts across the water, you see a brilliant flash of cobalt blue or a flick of emerald green.

The song is the trill of a whistle, a repetitive high-pitched 'chee' that in late spring is accompanied by an aerial chase of male after female. Eventually he strokes her with his bill. They nest in near-vertical tunnels that are lined with nothing more than fish bones. They like high-sided mud- or sandbanks and will fly some distance for a suitable breeding ground if there is not one near water. They like fresh water of all kinds – streams, canals, lakes, ponds, estuaries – as long as there is something suitable to sit on and watch for a catch.

For years I managed a large pond and never saw a single kingfisher, although it was teeming with newts. I would watch them on a nearby stream that was far harder to fish in. A birder pointed out that there was no perch, so I dragged a suitable bowed branch and planted it at the side. It looked ridiculous, like a giant fishing rod plonked there, but within days it had a kingfisher. I found her at the end of the summer, dead in the grass. Heartbroken, I buried her among some self-heal. I feel I can remember every kingfisher I've ever seen, but this is because sightings are rare, not the bird.

Since kingfishers are high in the food chain, they are vulnerable to the build-up of chemicals in rivers, pollution by industrial and agricultural products. This excludes the birds from many stretches of otherwise suitable rivers that would be habitats.

The canals are often perfect locations for kingfishers: deep, high banks suitable for nesting, plenty of overhanging branches and hidden spots to rest in, and a wealth of small fish. Once the canals' ecology settled to a point at which they started to clean themselves up, so the numbers of kingfishers began to rise.

20

Being in London made me realise how much I missed my garden in Birmingham. I had, if not happily then actively, walked away from the garden with all the paddling. The first touches of autumn brought on a keen sense in me that I should be harvesting, collecting seed, gathering up a summer's gardening that I sorely missed. It was time to settle back into the earth again, but I was in the wrong city to do that.

Along the London canals, I saw more of the weed I couldn't identify. It sprouted out of cracks in the edge of the canal-side and made its footing in the base of clumps of reed sweet-grass. I pinched the top off the mystery weed for reference before I left.

When I got home I consulted the *Collins Flower Guide*, the most complete guide to the flowers of Britain and Ireland. It's a joy to use if you know your families. The square stem and opposite leaves, without stipules, identify the weed as a member of the Lamiaceae family. It turned out to be gypsywort, *Lycopus europaeus*, a perennial of marshes, fens, wet woodlands, margins of rivers, canals, dykes, ponds and lakes. It was traditionally used by the Romani people to dye their linen and apparently their skin to mimic Egyptians in Europe, which seems rather far-fetched, the skin-dyeing rather than the linen. Anyway, that's how it got its common name. It is used in the treatment of premenstrual syndrome, thyroidism, against coughs and bleeding, as an astringent, narcotic, sedative and refrigerant – a disparate enough list for a straggly wayside thing.

The tip of the plant I'd saved for reference was dry and brittle from being stuck within the pages of a freshwater guide for naturalists. I tried rubbing it between my fingers to see the famous black dye but it shattered into fragments.

I'd come back to a wild, untamed garden. The night before, wind and rain had rattled the window panes, waking the dog and me. We would sit upright in bed and stare at the window, then at each other. Then the dog would nuzzle herself back under the blanket and fall asleep. I would listen to the gutters gurgle and splutter till I too drifted off, until the next burst. In the morning the garden was washed clean, the patio looked scrubbed, and as I picked my way through wet vegetation to get to the apple tree, I could hear the slugs munching and slurping. Still, for all it was a lost cause, the garden was having fun. The apple tree groaned with bright-red shiny fruit, all rather small because I'd failed to thin them, too many with the codling moth I hadn't trapped for. But there were a few perfect specimens, their perfume heady even on that wet, cool morning. I picked a bowlful for the house. After nine months or so of no apples, the first sweet, slightly greasy-skinned bright-red ones were such a treat that I gorged on them until the enamel on my teeth started to thin. After that there was a variety for each month till December, then another for storage. By February I'm usually out of home-stored ones, though my mother supplements them with a rather brilliant ancient cooker that fluffs up in the oven to a soufflé.

On a canal by the Olympic Park in London I found a sweet little apple, with distinct Cox genes, but people had picked most of them too early, ripping them off the twigs when they weren't ready to let go. They had torn the branches, too, so there were raw wounds down the trunk.

I'd travelled to Kazakhstan, the birthplace of the apple, the previous October to collect apple seeds. I had witnessed apples that spun and whirled down mountain white-waters and realised why they bobbed. The best apples we found in the Tian Shan mountains nearly always grew near streams, waterfalls or springs that burst forth to meet large, wider waters. A ripe apple can bob all the way to a new home and still be perfectly delectable for a bear, horse, mountain goat or wild sheep to eat and leave a perfect germination package behind.

When we were walking outside Almaty, in the foothills of the Tian Shan, we'd see bobbing apples sometimes a mile before we'd find the mother tree. Along the way we passed petroglyphs, hunting scenes of wild deer, tapped into the rock face and we'd find the apple eventually, which tasted exactly as you'd expect natural selection to taste. Generations of us and others, of deer and brown bears and wild horses, had chosen the sweetest, brightest apples to continue.

So, what of the generation that does not know when an apple is ripe, how to cup the fruit and push upwards to find out if the tree is ready to let go, that does not care to understand that pips removed too early from the tree will never ripen properly, and that relationships built on millennia of Silk Road traders, bears, horses, camels and even dung beetles quickly wither into unripe fruit on the ground?

* * *

Some days I met with leaps and bounds, but the leaps were few and the bounds far between. Many more days were conditioned by a deep, crippling introspection. I tripped between talking endlessly and hiding away. I wanted to be fierce, adventurous, spirited in my new relationship, but often I found myself clinging when I most needed to let go. I had never experienced before the often all-consuming desire not to leave someone. I had always been defined by independence in a relationship and now I felt crushed when I left Charlotte, unable to achieve much more than floating around in a boat, love-struck, punch-drunk and drifting till my next visit to her.

I got up early to spend the day afloat. I ran my finger over various maps, deciding which route to take. I had only a few big routes left to do before I had covered my city. I decided to head out to Dudley and chose Dudley Port as my destination station because I like the idea of there being a port in the middle of a landlocked city.

The train was empty. I sat in a row of side seats and watched the city rush past, a blur of green in the window to match the colour of the seats. I felt a bit empty, folded up, like the seats, torn, like their covers. I wondered if a day spent on my own was such a good idea, but I was there and determined to keep up the map I was making.

I'd spent the weekend slowly losing everything, including at times my sanity. It had started with unpacking yet another bag and ended with me howling on the bed, drowning in my panic, while the dog whimpered and my lover tossed around me, trying to talk sense back into the situation.

I'm not one to fall apart. I panicked and panicked at becoming needy and panicked, and panicked at my dry mouth, and panicked at the many anxious voices that all came out in one long and painful chorus.

I had felt, if not settled, at least relieved to be back in the green of Birmingham, to walk in the expansive parks, to feed the chickens and watch the bees, but sitting alone in the train, I felt that panic rise again.

At Dudley I got out and could see the canal on the other side of the rails. I had to go down from the platform, cross a road and climb all the way back up to get to the water. A sort of mist descended. Everything was very grey. A young heron stood and startled at my presence before reaching to the sky. I pumped up the boat against the grey, autumn's touches seeming subdued as if it couldn't quite be bothered.

I got onto the water and paddled a long, straight stretch. I played tag with the heron, noticed the ash keys and the first touches of red on the brambles. A small fish leapt ahead. The

Cut is high there, the city tumbles away, and there was that great expanse of sky. Yet because it was so grey it seemed to press down on the landscape. There were patches of exposed sandstone, an acid landscape of heathers, gorse and birch. It felt raw, and I noticed how cool the water was becoming, with just a thin sheet of plastic between me and it.

I passed several narrowboats and followed markers directing me to the city centre. It was eight miles away. The canal there was straight. I decided not to take the old line, which meandered to the city centre. What I thought was a tunnel would turn out to be a bend, but seeing my future mapped out with a grey sky and grey edges, I panicked and decided it was not the time to do this alone. I phoned my old friend Clare. She was finishing off a film script and we talked about writing, about how exposing it felt to put one word after another. We talked about love and about me and about her, then about me again. I felt like a broken record, stuck on a song I no longer wanted to sing. We agreed to meet for supper. I felt relieved at the thought of an old, dear friend's company. I felt buoyed by it, and because of that I phoned Charlotte. She did not feel buoyed: she felt bruised by the weekend. I floated, stopped paddling and tried not to feel panicked. I tried desperately to find the version of me that would be steady around this conversation. I tried to listen, but I couldn't always understand.

You cannot talk seriously on the phone and paddle, and you cannot float around and not paddle or you'll run into a narrowboat. In short, you cannot paddle and be present. Or: to be present on the phone to your lover you must not paddle.

We ended the conversation quietly. I could hear her voice echo in the concrete stairwell of her studio. I knew I shouldn't be demanding more time around this issue where talking wasn't going to get us anywhere. I wanted to run ahead. I wanted to race through the aftermath of coming out. I wanted to be a fully formed lesbian, even though I knew there was no such thing. I didn't want to erase my straight past: I was proud of my marriage

– I had been deeply happy, content, and it had brought me to where I was in many ways. It is my history. But I also felt trapped by the unsettled nature of my life. The steady, long-term relationship had afforded me great freedom. Now, perversely, that freedom, one of honesty, was so vast that at times it was overwhelming. I knew which path I wanted to be on, and I would wake often surprised that I felt no regret at coming out. I never thought, I must take this back. But I was scared of the unknown. I missed the security of my hidden nature.

I noticed mushrooms growing on the side of the canal. I wanted to be more interested in them or in the weeds or the damselfly that whizzed past. I want to peer at the waterside weeds and name all the liverworts and moss that covered the edges. Instead I was trapped inside me.

I lay back in the boat and allowed the grey sky to descend like a blanket. Then I noticed fireweed, or rosebay willowherb. It gained the first name because it likes to colonise burnt-out spaces, and famously turned post-war Britain into a blaze of pink. Its common name refers to the soft grey leaves that look like those of the willow. In late summer it is crowned with bright pink flowers, but in autumn it does something marvellous: it burnishes its fire-loving nature so that it looks like an autumn bonfire as those grey leaves turn red from the outer edge in, like burning embers, a brilliant orange-red, the seed heads wisping up like smoke. Here was a whole uninterrupted bank of colour, burning away. It was beautiful and fiery, unapologetic about its final call. It singed my retinas against all the grey gloom. Like a touch-paper, it lit up the bit of me that lives outside, and I remembered who I was and why I was there.

At the end of this blaze was the M5, its huge concrete bastions holding up a distant roar. Those cylinders were so vast I could paddle between them. The din of the motorway and the train line beside it made the place so deafening that it became almost peaceful. You could do things there you couldn't do elsewhere. So: I howled and howled and howled. I sobbed so loudly and so uncontrollably that I floated my boat along with nothing but a heaving chest. I clawed at the boat and at myself.

I cried in a manner far more unhinged than I can remember doing before. I outstripped the version of me that had howled on a station platform when I had first left Charlotte. I sobbed more violently than I had at the weekend or when I had left my marriage bed. I cried more angrily than I had when I was hurt by people's responses to the break-up and more vividly when I realised my own humility, that I might have mistaken myself. I cried, cried more, cried some and then I stopped. And I openly asked the little warrior out loud, without any embarrassment or hesitation, if she might like to retire now because I had suddenly understood something.

I'd been running on adrenalin for so long that I was exhausted. She had hauled me out of so much, held me up, enticed me around corners and pushed me forward when I wanted to hide. She'd put me on trains and taken me home again. She'd forced me through hospital doors and taken me out again. She'd been quite the maiden, loyal, strong, storming, but now I wanted to get on with life and she wasn't very good at the quiet stuff, the ordinary, the observed, so I howled to let her climb out again. And when she left, I promptly turned another corner on the canal, picked up the paddle and moved on.

It sounds farcical now, but in all the time I had been wandering around asking people to accept the new me, I hadn't asked the old me to do the same. I let go in all that howling. I have no idea if anyone heard me or saw the strange sight I must have made. But I let go, and once I had, I felt gloriously free.

I paddled from under the bridge and round a corner to find myself back in familiar territory. I passed under the Engine Arm Aqueduct and paddled down one of the toll islands covered with liverwort. This time the rain had sprung those folded sheets of brown back into life, and they glistened green. Many of them had their fruiting bodies, which look much like umbrellas. They are often known as umbrella or star-headed liverwort, *Marchantia polymorpha*. These were thallose liverwort, which look a little like miniature seaweed. They are dioecious, having separate male and female bodies. The tiny umbrellas are female; the male parts are small, stalked and have a flat disc on top – they look like flying saucers. There is a third body, the gemmae, a cup-shaped receptacle that is used for asexual reproduction. Inside the little cups are balls of cells, which are genetically identical to the parents. When rain splashes the contents of these tiny cups, the cells that will develop into new plants spill out. If the going is good, this asexual route is a way to colonise quickly, conquer new ground. And the shaded little island was just that, a space colonised by thousands of waving palm trees for Lilliputians, a thicket and forest for water bears to hunt in, a wondrous world to eyeball as I shunted past – there was little room for proper paddling between the island and the canal edge. I contemplated getting out and taking a hand lens to that world, but it was chilly in the shade and I suddenly felt hungry.

I moved out into the sun and made plans to meet my friend Emily for lunch. It was her birthday and, with little persuasion, I enticed her down to the Cut. I told her to bring some cans of cider, the sort we used to drink as teenagers, and we'd roll back twenty years and celebrate like kids.

I passed another abandoned toll island, this one in full sun. One end had partially collapsed, giving it two sorts of habitat, a marshy wetland and a dry-baked brick section. It's a wild little island, with stunted alders pushing through, bulrush and fireweed, toadflax and mint, hawkbit and snapdragons. I stopped to examine it more closely, hoping to find a terrestrial orchid, when a young man and his son stopped on the towpath. The young man waved and I turned to say hello. 'I was just telling my son here how we should get a boat, that it would be so peaceful out on the water, and there you are in a boat, looking so peaceful.' He grinned, and so did his son. I told him about the licence from the British Canoeing Association that allows you to go anywhere. 'Anywhere! That's wonderful. That's all the incentive we need. We'll get a boat,' he said. We discussed my boat and other blow-up boats. I told him about Ming and Sarah's Sevylor boat and added that you could often pick them up cheap on eBay. He was clearly so impressed that I found myself sitting up with pride in my funny red boat. I'd had amused and baffled, I'd had wary and inquisitive, but I'd not had someone outright admire my boat and me. I told them about the wildlife I'd seen – the huge pike I'd watched swim under the boat, the wild mint, the waterlilies and kingfishers. We parted, pleased with our meeting.

I paddled off daydreaming about their adventures. I imagined the young boy as a man, saying, 'Yeah, my dad used to take me paddling on the canals all the time. It was our thing we did together.' I imagined all sorts of people paddling there. As much as I'd loved the solitude, I also loved to meet other people out enjoying the water.

* * *

Ming brought me her skull collection, which is made up mostly of birds: owls, sea birds, song birds. There were ones she had found fleshed and buried till the earth had bleached them, there were damaged ones and ones fixed with superglue, and there was a heron's. She didn't find the heron's skull: it was a present from Sarah. Ming and Sarah love herons. They see them as their birds. They have a stuffed heron in a display case. And a crow Ming stuffed herself, a valiant first attempt at taxidermy. Ming is the first to point out its flaws – it is perhaps a little fat. There is also a freezer full of other dead things waiting to be stuffed. Ming is no longer accepting dead finds because there is a long backlog, including a gannet, an owl and, I think, maybe a hedgehog.

I looked at the heron, its razor-sharp beak seamlessly welded into its skull. Like all the stork family, the heron has a specialised spine that allows it to bend its neck back for flight and into an S shape ready to shoot out to seize prey. And shoot is exactly what they do. I have watched them fish from a standstill or walk slowly along a silted margin, carefully eyeing their meal. Mostly I see herons fishing, waiting to fish or digesting.

Less often, and thus much more rewarding, I see one preening. A heron does this regularly. It has a powder-down patch on its chest which it rubs its beak up and down until it's covered with a strange bloom. Then it carefully preens each feather. This cleans and re-waterproofs them. It is a careful, considered act that shouldn't be disturbed. The heron I watched preen for the longest time, eyed me sideways and I looked away, as one should for a lover when they are doing their hair. Admire, but admire carefully, for no one cares to be seen as vain.

* * *

Later, sitting at supper, I realised one of Charlotte's friends had exactly the same haircut as a female heron, a feathered quiff with a sharp undercut forming 'a crest down the middle of the crown, long, lanceolate feathers with long loose rami', the two back feathers being the longest. What with her sharp cheekbones and shy nature, I took to treating her much as I do the herons I meet, greeting them slowly, carefully and quietly so as not to disturb their territory. Next to the kingfishers on the water, the herons are my favourite finds. You might call her wife a kingfisher, bright and brilliant, with a darting humour and looks that everyone notices. In moments when I feel out of my depth, at parties or gatherings where I'm too wide-eyed and shy, I identify the others in the room as their wild counterparts, the birds and wayside plants I know well. Distilling the human world into the outdoor one I love steadies my nerve and gives me back just enough confidence to stay put. Often I feel like those herons I play tag with, always one flight away.

* * *

Soon I spotted my friend Emily walking in the afternoon sun, her trench coat golden in the light. With sunglasses and gold sandals, she looked far too glamorous for the Cut. Emily and I met when I worked for the BBC. I liked her from the minute I met her. I remember she was wearing a skirt and sandals and, despite her tiny stature, she helped me haul a huge potted palm tree into the back of a van as if it took little more effort than lifting up a shopping bag. She was full of hidden surprises and had become a dear friend to both H and me. Our separation had not been easy for her and, with the added distance of our living in separate cities, we saw far too little of each other.

She waved a couple of cans and I waved back, not that I needed to make myself noticed. Another towpath user turned to stare, bemused by the sight of us both. Although I had my bike strapped to the front of the boat, I persuaded Emily that we could both get into it and I'd paddle her to the glass factory. There's no pedestrian route, and the disused boat hulls would make an excellent spot to sun ourselves and drink cider. She didn't even hesitate to question two people and a bike in a one-person boat and gamely jumped in. We both had to do the octopus move, throwing our legs over the edge of the raft to lighten the load on the floor. This made kayaking impossible, so I split the paddle in half and we canoed slowly down the Main Line. The boat sat so low in the water beneath our weight that my feet lapped the surface and we giggled our way round the bend.

I moored up to one of the old butty barges and hauled myself, our bags, the cider and eventually Emily up onto a rusting hull. There are several moored up together. One had completely sunk in the time I'd been going there. Another was full of water and made an appealing pool. Further down, a third was crowded with water plants; the flowering rush had bloomed there earlier and now bulrushes swayed, their seed heads disintegrating in the wind to colonise new ground. They made the perfect urban ponds. We sat on the edge of the hull peering into the rust-coloured water and drank the cider. The day was hot and empty.

With no other boats around, only the boom of the metal-pressing factory reminded us we were not alone. It was a perfect urban playground, perfect for catching up on gossip, for discussing life, perfect for a spontaneous afternoon's adventure. I remember it clearly because it was such a happy, easygoing few hours, but I didn't know then how rare that would be. I was still lightheaded from all that howling, and a little naïve, perhaps even arrogant, not to expect more tumbling. I didn't know that you often have to unravel completely before you can start to work your yarn back into something solid to carry on.

21

I don't remember what happened after that. Those days are lost now, although I remember dipping in and out of anxiety attacks. They would leave me breathless on the floor, then crawling up for air. They went on for months, leaving me clueless as to where I was, wandering around the tube map, getting off at stations to rerun my journey, leaving me sprawled across Marylebone station ticket office, coins splayed out around me, trying to concentrate on what the police officer was saying.

Charlotte would appear at the end of the road, at the top of an escalator, off a plane, off a train, with a cup of tea, a bowl of soup or a drawn bath. I was so anxious in those periods that I wouldn't let her go, imploring her to let me stay longer. I would claw and tear at any spare air between us. I felt I had endless motion sickness – I was neither leaving nor arriving.

I had lost H. I had let go.

Charlotte was so alive, there was no reason to hold on. There was no need to. Every day, every hour there was an adventure, some part to be seized, and she did it. I sat in my metaphorical boat, washed by waves, which took me just close enough to cling to her but eventually broke my hold so that I washed back again.

I was not used to feeling attachment like that. I was used to being free-spirited and independent. I was used to getting lost in detail, in the other world of other things, and suddenly my detail-oriented self was gone. I tried to concentrate on the pavement plants: chicory, sow thistle, toadflax, bonfire moss, candelariella, pearlwort, corydalis, pennywort, foxgloves, front door, home.

Then one day I found H in our room sorting through files, beginning to pack up to move out. I asked him about his future, what he would do next about operations and hospital treatments. We both knew what lay ahead. I wanted to do the right thing, but I wanted more badly to be let go. He said what I couldn't say: 'I don't want you there because I can't rely on you. You are no longer emotionally involved in the way you were when you were my wife. Therefore I won't rely on you.'

I bristled. 'I will be there.'

'You may be there, but you won't be wholly there. You don't have the same investment. It's not the same.'

I felt broken. I didn't feel relief. I didn't argue back. I didn't try to make my case. I didn't beg. I said nothing. I just stood in the corner of the room and felt very small.

*　　*　　*

Sarah, Ming and I agreed to go for a long paddle when we saw the forecast was offering one of those lingering early-autumn evenings. We set off late and ended the paddle in the dark. It was a breathtaking journey from start to finish.

Sarah and Ming had been going on about the canal up by the water park in Tamworth for some time and, although it took me out of the city and thus was not strictly part of my adventure's remit, I wanted to be in the countryside and there was the promise of a good pub at the end of the paddle. Mostly I wanted to be with them. I hadn't seen them for two weeks and I keenly missed their company.

I met Sarah in town and we headed out. The traffic stalled, then crawled, leaving us plenty of time to talk. I told her about my week in Scotland with Charlotte, of walking to see violent whirlpools, of icy swims in the sea and dyke swarms, which are when several thousand geological dykes appear. Arran is famous for its Kildonan dyke swarm.

We met Ming in the van, dropped the car off at the endpoint of the paddle, then drove back six miles or so to get into the water. We had company as we blew up the boat: a young couple smoking fags and a fisherman with a couple of cans, hoping to catch some roach. They were jolly company, laughing at our antics, taking pictures of our boats, and we paddled off in high spirits. This is a lovely stretch because there are numerous passenger bridges, beautiful old brick constructions, crumbling and worn in places, glowing in the evening sun. They mark rights of way from before the canal was built and were often made with the bare minimum of bricks so the narrowboats have to squeeze through them. Some have tiny rooms at their buttresses, with a tiny hobbit door and a window with medieval-looking bars. They look neither big enough to sleep in, nor that useful as storage. As I passed through I imagined what someone might want to put in them, tools perhaps, for maintaining the canal, or food – they would certainly remain cool.

Without the bike and carrying the bare minimum of luggage, I was fast and, for once, I outstripped the girls. Sarah demanded that we all slow down and take a more leisurely attitude to the glorious evening. We stopped to forage for damsons and black-berries, shared a beer and clambered over a couple of locks, dragging the boats and trying not to spill the last of the beer.

We passed outside the last of the suburbs and were in country-side. The fields rolled away from the canal and there were moments when the sky spread below us, like wings, and our spirits soared. We stopped to talk to a couple moored up on their narrowboat. They asked where we'd come from and we pointed back to the city and asked them the same thing. Their accents were southern, Sarah guessed Kent, and the conversation babbled along in a jolly manner. On retirement, they had packed up all their belongings, sold their house and bought a boat. Eleven years on, with no permanent mooring, they meandered around the waterways, spending the winters near cities for convenience. They were heading up towards Liverpool after a summer spent floating around. If you don't have a permanent mooring, you can spend fourteen days in one spot before you have to move on. Two weeks, they had decided, was enough time to spend anywhere. Their easy conversation and obvious happiness with their floating life were infectious. The sun was setting and we still had miles to go, so we pushed off, wishing them well, marvelling that two people could live in such close quarters so happily.

We passed delightful edges of reeds, flowering rush, arrowheads and reed sweet-grass. We floated past waterlily patches and ancient hedgerows. We passed a modern pub with a loud wedding party: small children hung along the fence in their party dresses, squealing with delight as we floated past.

We meandered out of the open fields into high-sided banks of beech and oak with sandstone outcrops; those dark tunnels of green in the last of the dappled sun were breathtaking. We came to a tunnel, just long enough to obscure the other end, and paddled through the water, sloshing and sucking as our paddles hit the side. The tunnel opened out into an amphitheatre of trees that rose above the canal and bathed the basin in inky green light. The water was littered with leaves, and a huge dead tench, bloated, bobbed along. I prodded it with my paddle and its scales sluiced of. Although it's long gone, my gesture still seems painful. We stopped to look at it for a bit, then paddled on. A slow burn began to creep up my arms, yet Sarah thought we still had at least three miles to go. On land and your feet, you can't conceive of how slow and long a mile can feel when you're dragging yourself by your arms.

We paddled into a section with a long mud bank full of hawthorn, hazel, blackthorn and sloes. It was punctuated with small tunnels, a perfect kingfisher bank, long and deep, and we slowed to watch for any sign of activity. We saw long-tailed tits, robins and finches, but no brilliant blue flashes. I went on ahead to buy myself some time so that I could rest for a few minutes.

Along the bank, I caught a flash and a dip and shouted to the girls to catch up as there was a kingfisher, but it was gone in its blue flash. Further along, I spotted another two as the sun set, turning the water into liquid copper that oxidised into its green patina. As the last of the sun went down, the bats appeared, and our final stretch to the pub was as poetic as a paddle could be as they flitted around us, swooping in front of the boats' wakes. The trees turned into line drawings in the gloaming and everything seemed magical: what had been wood might now be a dragon or a Green Man charging, arms up, to the water.

We neared the pub as the last light was going and called to the barmaid to find out if they were still serving food. We would just make last orders. We dragged ourselves out, still chatting to the barmaid as we packed up the boats. When she left, Sarah said, 'I reckon she's on our team,' and I felt a sudden rush of acceptance as gay. It was a small thing, but it mattered greatly to me every time anyone confirmed it.

* * *

We ate hearty pub fare, pie and chips, scampi and chips, curry and chips, and drank hoppy beer sitting outside the very pretty Georgian pub, alongside the canal, watching the bats swoop and the inky night take over.

We were pleased with ourselves for making it so far, pleased to be out of the city, pleased that it could all be quite so charming. We drove Ming back to the van and Sarah drove me home. We continued to talk about love right to my front door, where I clambered out, exhausted, yet so happy. A very ordinary catching of happiness that I would hold onto, or its memory, in weeks to come when my world rolled around again and I tried to keep a steady pace.

22

I might have been at peace for once, but I was worn out. Too much travelling, too much paddling, and I'd picked up a chest infection. I was hacking with a foul cough and felt weak. Within days, I had passed it to H. This made things fraught, putting him back on more rounds of antibiotics, my guilt meaningless. I was run down and to blame for bringing germs into the house.

In the single bed in my study, I looked down on the garden. From this eyrie it looked romantically dishevelled, but I knew otherwise. The garden was an easy prop. It had held me afloat when sinking might have made more sense. As long as it was flourishing, perhaps no one would notice I wasn't. I had hidden behind H's illness; I had hidden behind my pretty garden.

My garden was no longer pretty – well, not in any conventional sense. It was a mess with giant holes and too many wild, wayward weeds. It was crawling with fat slugs that munched its lushness. The apple trees were bent double with the weight of their bounty; the quince swayed uneasily with its burden; the rose rambled into corners it had never previously been allowed to explore. The Jerusalem artichokes marched outwards and the wild strawberries danced into every spare spot.

Anything that liked to seed itself into new territory did so shamelessly, and the path no longer existed. Down at the bottom by the compost, you could crouch between all the growth and hide away for ever. It was not a garden any more. It had gone feral, was on the way to being wild, true to itself. And every time I looked upon that space, it felt too much like the whirl that was my heart.

But I had to walk away. I had to let it go. If I no longer allowed it to prop me up I would move forward to define my new self. It had to grow wild, so that I could, too, and together we would both find a new way. I'd seen the same thing happen when my mother lost her twin sister.

As my mother retreated in grief, her walled garden grew grand in its escape. Everyone who wandered through it and saw roses dripping from ancient apple trees or blossom tumble over the beds and into the path, or who picked their way over carpets of fallen petals and pushed past asparagus flowering in triumph, marvelled at the party the garden was throwing in the absence of its owner. My mother barely glanced at it. She sat by a TV and watched black-and-white footage of her childhood over and over again, as if she might be able to drain the world outside of colour. She raged. She cried and howled and crawled and moaned. Outside, the roses went their merry way with the bees, and the hips grew fat in response.

* * *

Charlotte called me. At this point I had never talked to her on the phone at home. We had never strayed beyond fleeting phone conversations. We had stuck to the safety of the written word in clipped text form. Now we were talking on the phone because we both needed to hear emotion. We were terrified, I think, by the realisation that this heady first flush of love was a thin veil for something else. We had filled our time with lust as if to push out the intensity of the next stage.

I was pulling wildly at bindweed, yanking it out with everything that it had twirled around, as I tried to hide my emotion, and she was slowing me down so she could hear its song. I was very afraid that if she saw me in that wild space, tugging at bindweed, bloodied from thorns, reddened by ant bites, smeared in slug slime, dusted in dirt, she might just understand how close to the edge I was. Pulling at the bindweed, talking at the same time as trying to listen, trying not to cling while I sank among all those weeds. Trying desperately to be someone who didn't look like that messy garden. I failed. I drifted off and her voice became faint.

The following day she flew away to work. I woke after a night of heavy rain and decided it was time to tackle some of that wild space. I cut back astrantias and the geranium, 'Mrs Kendal Clarke', that was taking over the path. I deadheaded the snotty tissues of spent roses and pulled at the spidery wild strawberries, sending out in their web an army of youngsters. I pretended I had energy while my chest raged away.

H's anger swelled at the injustice of catching my chest infection. I didn't know how to negotiate this next bit, of separating. I felt he was reliant on me to stay and care, yet I was the one person he wanted to be away from. Promising to care had eased my guilt, but confronted with his anger I wasn't sure I wanted to do it. I wanted to run away but my weak chest wouldn't let me. I wanted to run from everyone. I fantasised about taking my small boat to the coast to float between tiny wild islands. I pretended I wasn't terrified about how we'd finally separate, when he'd move out, where he'd go.

*   *   *

Charlotte flew back, but instead of going home, she came straight to me. She booked a hotel room and sat me on a great white bed of pressed Egyptian cotton and ordered room service. When I insisted on turning away or talking to the window, she firmly turned me back, handed me tissues and unwrapped the twining bindweed from round my neck and the web of strawberry runners from my mouth, and pulled out the thorns in my fingers.

I knew then that she wasn't going anywhere, however messy my situation was, and for that night I let go of every fight within me.

* * *

I came home expecting to take H to hospital with an infection I had given him. I came home guilty. I came home, but it wasn't that any more. He didn't need to go into hospital this time. I felt relieved, then guilty for feeling relieved.

I went out into the garden to cut chives for a sandwich – I'd wanted to get Welsh onions, but they had disappeared in the mess. On the patio, I disturbed a small male blackbird. It was eating a slug. I'm such a terrible gardener now, I thought. I can't even time my pest control right. I looked around to make up for this and spotted huge cultivated blackberries, fat and blistering in the humidity. The bramble had garlanded itself along the honeysuckle and into the vine, which had young grapes by the thousand. Not such a bad gardener then, I concurred, then picked the ripest blackberries and tossed them to the blackbird, which inquisitively turned his head to one side as if he was as confused about my role as I was.

He did that funny blackbird thing of running around the blackberry to check it out. The pecked slug was writhing in pain; the blackberry was bleeding from the thud. The blackbird plucked up the huge berry and ran towards the steps, took three jaunty hops and ran to a considered safe spot behind the chives.

Not only had I ruined pest control, I'd lost the moment to collect the chives. I stood on the slug to put it out of its misery and found a snail which I left by its side in case the blackbird wanted seconds.

I looked to see where the blackbird was. It turned its head to me and its beak was smeared with purple juice. If blackbirds grin, then that was what he was doing. I asked aloud, 'Can I cut chives?' but the blackbird wasn't there for such communion. It cared not for the rest of the conversation and flew off. I picked my chives and ate them in a cheese sandwich.

*　　*　　*

We did not go to hospital the next day or the day after. All week we danced around the subject, waiting to see the next move.

A man came to value our house so that we could remortgage and H could move out. This isn't like having your house valued by an estate agent. No one admires all the work you've done, your period restoration, the parquet floor – it had nearly killed me and put H in hospital. No one says, 'Isn't the garden lovely/sunny/full?' or whatever polite people say about a garden that is going wild. Instead a man in a crisp blue shirt and practical I-stand-all-day shoes came and did precise line drawings on graph paper, peered into cupboards and took endless pictures of windows and doorways. He didn't want coffee or tea or conversation.

For some reason I felt compelled to point out how many apples there were going to be this autumn or how fat the figs were, that there would be so many bunches of grapes to juice and that the cultivated blackberry was bursting with so many berries that you could share them with any blackbird that passed and still have plenty for tea. I wanted to say, 'This is how rich I am. This is the meaning of home.'

Instead, I sat quietly in the sitting room and, for want of something to do, read *Drawn and Quarterly 25: Twenty-five Years of Contemporary Cartooning, Comics and Graphic Novels.* I read a story by Debbie Drechsler about getting an abortion. So much was held in the blue and black lines, yet so little was said in words. That is the comic book's genius: in an amazingly short space, in just a few strokes or lines, a whole world of emotion is portrayed.

I looked up at the man making a line drawing of my house. A drawing that would go into a file among thousands of others.

But those few lines held no emotion, told no tales, just the sum of who we had been to be divided up and moved on.

When he had gone, I wanted to go too. I wanted to go to the water, but my chest was still weak and I knew that paddling would exhaust me and prolong the battle. I went to the allotment instead. The afternoon was warm and I sowed lettuce, kale, kailaan and corn salad. I sowed as a protest to all the change. I sowed to ground myself to that place even though just then I didn't always recognise it as home. And then, after sowing and hoeing, I found myself lulled back into a rhythm. I deadheaded, pottered, pulled weeds and ordered the mess into something still wild but productive. After a few hours, I looked back on my work and I saw somewhere familiar again. Despite my neglect and my haphazard sowing, there were beans to pick, potatoes to dig up, tomatoes swelling on tangled vines – and, if you got down close to the ground, little things, tiny carrots and Hamburg parsley, fine fronds of fennel and baby beets, were appearing. Seeds scattered in a foreign past that had lain dormant and were only just starting up now, as if the allotment had known I'd be back.

23

I traced over my green ink on my faded All Day map of Birmingham, peering for the last few routes. There were a few miles to do here and there, mostly in the north-west corner of the map, and a few treasured routes I wanted to do again in the dead of winter, but mostly my map was finished. I called Dave and asked if he wanted to go for a celebratory paddle and, if so, did he have anywhere in mind? He texted back, suggesting the Bumble Hole Branch Canal. It was officially outside my city, in the Black Country, but it was such a wonderful name that I waived that detail.

The Bumble Hole is a water-filled clay pit that is now a nature reserve. Originally, it formed part of the Dudley No. 2 Canal, but in 1858 the swanky Netherton Tunnel was opened, bypassing both the Bumble Hole and the Dudley Canal. These days, you can get to the Netherton Tunnel from the Bumble Hole.

We set off on a Saturday morning and drove to a somewhat dull 1970s housing estate with one brilliant front garden full of over-the-top dahlias and an old man tending them carefully. Dave's vintage sports car looked completely at odds parked there, as did we carrying our boats down a grass bank to the canal. There was a beautiful disused aqueduct sprouting a fringe of green trees, and several basins with water so crystal clear that you could see straight to the bottom and watch the little fish flutter through the hornwort. I pondered briefly whether this would be a place to come swimming – these tiny basins looked like perfect natural swimming ponds as long as you didn't kick up the polluted bottoms.

A boy and his dad were posted on one of the iron bridges about to start fishing, but otherwise the place was deserted. Just a few metres from dull suburbia and what would once have been a black-smoke industrial hell-hole was now a rural idyll, so thick with textured greens and the first touches of autumn that it was quite hard to believe we were in Dudley, the butt of all bad-accent-mimicking jokes.

We blew up our boats next to Park Head Junction, which has three locks and splits Dudley No. 1 Canal from Dudley No. 2 Canal. Canal No. 1 was built by the unscrupulous Lord Dudley of Dudley Tunnel fame to take the Birmingham Cut at Tipton into his coal and limestone mines. Dudley No. 2 Canal was built to the right of the original to join up with the Birmingham Canal at Selly Oak, via the Lappal Tunnel, and was a fairly unsuccessful attempt at breaking the mighty Birmingham Canal's monopoly. The canal is long gone, though a group of volunteers are determined to resurrect it. If this sounds farcical it is not: in the 1970s so much of the British canal network was in decline that many canals were no longer passable, often filled with shopping trolleys and barely enough water to fill a ditch. Nearly every one was cleared, restored and re-dug by dedicated volunteers working by hand.

I launched my boat quickly and paddled to the other side of the basin to see if I could find anything lurking in the reeds. Dave was slower, and after a while he called me back. I paddled over to see what the issue was. Great big Dave, all six foot two of him, was wary of getting into the water. I moved my boat close to his, not that it did anything to steady it, just offered support, I guess. I'd become so used to throwing my boat and myself onto the water that I'd forgotten it felt unnatural. Often the canal was a good foot or more beneath the towpath and you had to launch yourself into your boat, regardless that its bottom was just a thin layer of wobbly plastic. Once Dave was in, we started off and immediately ran into a narrowboat. A woman on board asked curtly if more of us were coming and I felt a prick of leisure-boat rivalry. The same pinch I feel when car drivers make out it's a huge effort to get out of the way of a bike. I wanted to shout, 'I am my engine', but instead I just shook my head and paddled on defiantly, with Dave behind.

We quickly got into a rhythm and passed down a tunnel of green with a towpath to the right. We met a few friendly dog-walkers and cyclists, a little surprised to see us, then ran into a gang of young boys on bikes off fishing. They shouted to us, wanting us to let them have a go. They were filthy and cheeky and delightful, and would clearly have pinched the boats for a joy ride if they could. I told them that their bikes were not a good enough substitute, and they tried other lines of bargaining before giving up and cycling off. Dave laughed. 'Yours might just be the first posh accent on these canals those boys have ever heard – a posh bird in a boat on the Cut.'

We paddled on, the Cut ablaze with autumn colour as all the dogwoods, *Cornus sanguinea*, glowed ember red. An American visiting the Black Country in 1869 wrote that it was 'black by day and red by night', referring to all the coal burning. The dogwoods, with their black berries and brilliant autumn reds, seemed a fitting plant to adorn the edges.

The Black Country does not get its name because of the smog, although it was famously one of the dirtiest, most polluted places of the industrial revolution, but because of what it lay upon: a thick vein of coal, one of the largest in the country. Snaking along the canal, the Black Country limestone hills rise and fall, giving way to spectacular views of its geology. It's one of great variation. Over time tectonic plates have folded and broken the strata, creating Dudley's fine hills, leaving vast sheets where ancient volcanic eruptions blew molten magma into chambers that cooled towards basalt rock. Over this, there is red sandstone, pebble beds, old mud and glacial deposits. It's a geologist's dream, regularly throwing up new species of fossils in the limestone folds.

Around a bend, we met a heron and played tag with it. I have learnt that it is almost impossible to get up close to a heron as they are too wary, unless you find one fishing for something worthwhile, when they'll take a risk and linger. Dave and I talked about heronries. There's a large one in the ponds at Cannon Hill. Heronries are much like their owners, elusive things that you stumble upon. I find it fascinating that such a big bird is so easily lost. We found the heron sitting on the Boshboil Arm Bridge, made by the Toll End Works, a fine bit of local cast-iron work against a steel-grey sky. The heron took off, and I snapped a photo, catching the bird reaching high for the heavens.

We passed under Astle Bridge, named after the Baggies' – West Bromwich Albion's – and thus Dudley's, most famous player, Jeff Astle. When he died, at fifty-nine, he couldn't remember his past glories, or even that he had been a footballer. He had sustained traumatic head injuries as a result of heading a football too much. The footballs in his day were made of thick leather and, when wet, extremely heavy. He was an extremely good header. At the height of his career someone graffitied 'ASTLE IS KING' under what was then Primrose Bridge. The council removed it but after several days it reappeared. The game went on and on until locally no one remembered that the bridge had been named after a flower: it had become Astle's Bridge. After his death and a considerable campaign, the bridge was officially renamed. There is still some graffiti declaring him king.

We headed on to Highbridge Road Bridge. This was once the second highest canal bridge in the land and became a notorious suicide spot during the depression of the 1930s. It's locally known as the Sounding Bridge because its echo is so lovely. Once it wasn't a bridge at all but a legging tunnel, the sort where there was no towpath and men had to walk the narrowboats, through lying on the roof of their boat. This is a slow process and as canal engineering progressed, the tunnel was blasted through and the fine, high-arched bridge built instead. The exedra of the tunnel is still visible, as are fine strata of sandstone, conglomeratic (pebble bed) bases and coal deposits as well as a basalt dyke.

The oldest rocks were formed on the seabed 400 million years ago when the whole area was a shallow sea. During the Devonian period the land rose and became a vast tropical rainforest, the dead vegetation compressing and compressing until it became coal and the visible vein of red sandstone. Among the strata are basalt dykes, once blistering columns of rising magma from active volcanoes deep within the earth. Dykes are easy to spot because they cut across the norm. If everything else is horizontal, dykes are vertical. They do the opposite of the standard formation. For obvious reasons, I love dykes.

The dykes are known as an 'unconformity' in geological terms. An unconformity is a break or hiatus in the sedimentary geological record, which usually occurs when one sediment erodes before it is buried under sediments deposited during a later period. As this isn't consistent, it means the timeline looks all wrong: older rock can appear on the surface with younger rock below. That baffled geologists and made establishing the age of the earth very hard. That is, until an eighteenth-century Scottish geologist called James Hutton came to ponder the issue. He noticed that unconformity was the pattern and began to work out why it might happen. He did this at about the same time as the Brewin Tunnel was blasted open to make the bridge and move the boats faster through to Birmingham. Unconformities, much like coal extraction, changed the world for ever. They proved that the earth is much older than the Bible suggested. Hutton's theory of unconformity made him the founding father of modern geology.

I know this because falling in love required me to go on that geology walking tour of Arran with Charlotte, where I mostly failed to grasp the geology because I spent my time hunting for wild plants and was often out of earshot. However, I found some very rare wintergreens growing at the base of one of Hutton's unconformities at the tip of Arran so that bit of the lecture stuck.

We lingered, discussing the geology and taking pictures, before pushing on. I hadn't imagined that I might fall in love with the water in different seasons, but autumn was seducing me. Paddling between buttery leaves, those that are burnt umber or with a blood-red glow or coppery, with the slight chill of the water beneath and the smell of it on your hands, that slightly dank metallic smell, and the need to keep paddling before the chill crept up from beneath me, made me realise how much I loved being on the water. That song-of-the-paddle thing is true. Kayaking was working its way into my bones, like walking and cycling and pushing my fingers deep into the earth. Suddenly I knew I wouldn't give it up.

Round the corner we found Lodge Farm Reservoir, a flooded canal pit originally used to top up the canal, though now you're more likely to find people sailing on it. Later on, we stopped paddling to take in the views. A thin slice framed by a modern housing estate allows you to see across the valley onto the wooded Wychbury Hill. If you frame out the houses, you could be up a mountain in Italy or somewhere far and remote. It was an unexpected view in an area known for its ugly town planning. On the hills behind sits a medieval church, its tower waving a red-and-yellow flag, and we stopped to eat the cakes I had brought along. We tethered our boats together and I divvied up the two cakes. I was unbothered about eating with wet canal hands. I'd ingested plenty of that filthy water on many trips and lived to tell the tale, but Dave, with his environmental health officer hat on, was rightly wary. Later I saw a dead rat, bloated, its fur peeling off, as if someone had shaved it with the sharpest of cutthroat razors. I thought he probably had a point.

We wolfed the cakes and took in the widening basin on the far side of a Proving House, where anchors and chains were tested for strength. It had a white-painted anchor outside, commemorating the huge anchor and chain required for the *Titanic*. We were now paddling into heavy industry. There were numerous sites of iron works, stations and disused factories.

We passed moorings that came with their own island so that each boat had a small allotment-like space to hang out washing, eat out and garden. If it wasn't for giving up a decent space to grow things, I could be attracted by the boating life, but this looked like the perfect solution. There was even a social club.

Around there, I smelt the distinct whiff of death and found it under a willow. It initially looked like a log, but I decided it must be a giant pike rotting away, little bits of skin and flesh flaking off. I was tempted to poke it but, after Dave's health and safety lecture about eating food with canal hands, I thought I shouldn't. A small child and her grandfather were pleased to see us and we waved our paddles as she gleefully chattered incomprehensibly.

We took the Bumble Hole Branch Canal up to Harris's boat-yard, which has permanent moorings. It's one of the only working boatyards around there. It had a very pretty timber structure that wouldn't now look out of place in the Deep South of the United States, with its tin signs and wooden chairs on the porch, ready for a beer. It had a rather lovely timber, fallow-style dockside crane and a pretty view across the Bumble Hole.

We returned to the main canal and ran into the tour boat from the Black Country Museum, packed with couples in macs who waved to us. We let them moor up at the Bumble Hole nature reserve visitors' centre before us, then came to our senses: we'd never get a cup of tea if we let them order first. We hurried in. It was delightfully old-fashioned, with a row of second-hand books and bric-à-brac to sell, and a cabinet of taxidermy animals from the canal. I studied the heron as I waited to order tea, and some rather tatty but informative posters on the history of Bumble Hole and its association with the *Titanic*.

Bumble Hole took its name from a local legend that the industrialist who owned the clay pit had a steam-driven hammer, which made a *bum-hul bum-hul* sound and became known as 'bum-hul in the hole', which sounds like a dubious joke some might make at the pub. Still, I'm glad it stuck.

I ordered Dave a cup of tea and a watery, sweet hot chocolate for myself. I also bought several biscuit bars of a variety I was quite sure was no longer made. Dave and I discussed the various merits of childhood sweet treats between bouts of canal history as I picked his brains for answers to some questions I'd accumulated about the canals.

After we'd squeaked our teeth on the polystyrene cups and licked the crumbs from the wrappers we decided to look at the nature reserve, then paddle up to the Netherton Tunnel. Here we met an angler fishing for perch. He pulled out tiny fish, which he examined, then threw back in before wandering on.

Dave and I discussed the great crack in the brickwork of the Netherton Tunnel and debated whether we'd want to go home via the tunnel but decided it would take too long.

As we sat in our boats peering into its dark recesses, we could see a tiny dot of white light at the end. Dave told me that Louise and her friends would dare each other to run as far as they could into the tunnel because, as with all tunnels of such length, that little white dot is an illusion. Get a mile in and the tunnel is centre-of-the-earth dark and terrifying. We saw two kids on BMX bikes egg each other on to go down the tunnel without lights, another generation upholding a fine Black Country tradition.

We decided to turn back. I always dread the return journey a little. I often leave it too late when I'm already too weary or too hungry, and I fear knowing the route and how long it will take. But the reality is different. The weather often changes the water, a whip of wind here, a push there, and that return trip was no different.

I kept my eye open for the huge dead pike, but it was gone from under the willow when we turned around the bend. I wondered if something had dragged it under to gobble it up. I wondered, as I always do, about what eats the floating dead animals, if they eat everything or whether bones are buried deep in the toxic sludge at the bottom. I resent having company when I find dead things, because I like to poke about and see how they are put together. Ever since I'd seen Ming's skull collection, and the beautiful arrowhead of the heron, I'd been hankering for one of my own. I had many dead rat skulls I'd collected over the years and a few from rabbits, but I'd realised that my collection lacked ambition.

A quarter of a mile on I could smell the carcass: the wind and slight underwater current had pulled it along so that now it floated in the middle of the canal. I badgered Dave to come and look at the huge dead pike. When we got up close, the flesh on the head had all but been removed. A great thick body of rotting muscles, skin and fat remained, but the head was raw bone and nothing else. Dave pointed out that it was not a pike – there was no jutting lower jaw and it had a fin that was almost the length of its body. It bumped between our boats and flesh flaked off. It smelt as death does: sweet, obnoxious and lingering.

We stared at it and Dave declared it an eel. An eel. I wanted it. I wanted to drag its flaking, putrid body behind the boat and bury it, only to dig it up in a month's time and wonder at it. An eel. I'd thought the pike had my heart for being the best beast below. But this eel was as thick as my thigh and at least four feet long. It had looked initially like a floating plank. It was pretty foul dead, but alive it would have been terrifying. I wanted to swim in these canals? This eel was a game-changer. Sorry, pike, you've been trumped by something far more seductive, I thought. I looked at Dave, who was showing signs of retching, and knew that the canal-water-is-gross lecture was not far behind, so I let the eel flake away from us.

How did he know there were eels in the canal? Had he seen one before? Was this one typical? How had it got there? I badgered him. He said he was confident that the canal was full of eels. I disbelieved him. Eels migrate: how would they get into a canal?

We paddled past two young anglers and I asked if they caught eels. If so, were there many? One replied that they often caught eels, sometimes as long as our boats, and there were known to be larger ones. That, yes, the canal was full of eels.

Once we'd left them, Dave admitted that he was a bit of an eel enthusiast. Now, when he admits he likes something, he's also admitting he has a vast and profound understanding of it. He has a brain that can leap and collect and disseminate and round back again before you've started to grasp the concept. So I settled back into my boat, found an easy rhythm to my paddle and waited to hear all about the eel.

* * *

When I think of eels, I think of that scene in *The Tin Drum*. It revels in the revoltingness of eels. Oskar's mother, Agnes, is on the beach with two men; one is her cousin and lover, Jan, the other Oskar's presumptive father, Alfred Matzerath. There is also an old man, pulling something out of the sea. It is a rotting horse's head that is writhing with eels. Matzerath helps him by bringing a bag, which we learn is full of salt: the eels will wriggle to death, and the salt will remove the slime. In the book, this practice is noted as illegal, but the old man does it anyway.

The old man pulls two eels from the throat of the rotting horse and this causes Agnes to throw up her breakfast and Oskar to play his toy drum incessantly. Jan goes to Agnes, but the scene quickly descends into something grotesque and muddied by the strange reverie that this story revels in. Instead of helping Agnes, Jan feels her arse. She throws up some more. The eels writhe around the rotting carcass, Matzerath is more interested in eating the eels than he is in his wife, and Oskar's drumming heightens it all – the squirming, sick-filled rottenness of modernity.

It was not until years after I'd watched this film that I could look at live eels without wanting to retch.

There are eel racks on the River Test near my parents' home. They were once common all over the UK because eels were so common. There are medieval records showing that eels were used as currency. In the early 2000s eels could fetch up to £600 a kilo, gold coins running up rivers. Ancient gold coins, for the eel has an interesting tale to tell, one of bio-geography, scientific mystery, climate change and some dubious political and business interests.

Although eels are indigenous to the British Isles, all of them were spawned in the Sargasso Sea. Their life cycle is extraordinary and spans the ocean. They start life as flat, transparent larvae, known as leptocephali. They drift in the surface waters of the sea, eating small particles of biological debris, dead and dying animals, plankton, faecal matter, sand, soot and bacteria known as marine snow. It will take them up to a year, sometimes longer, to travel from the Sargasso Sea to European coastal waters. They look much like transparent willow leaves and can swim between one and five miles an hour using the Gulf Stream to whip across the ocean. Once in European water they will metamorphose into glass eels, still transparent but with red gills and their heart now visible. It's a transitional position between the ocean and fresh water, an intermediary stage before pigmentation occurs. Glass eels enter the Thames en masse, migrating up rivers and streams. Life is precarious, but their transparency helps, and they still like to pretend they are leaves.

The glass eels are known to climb out of the water and will flatten themselves to look like a blade of grass to hide from herons, who pluck them out of the water for tea. Weirs and flood barriers pose a threat to glass eels: smooth-sided engineered rivers are not easy to pass. The Thames now has a number of eel passes, bristled brushes that allow the eels to climb out of the water and wriggle along to the next stage.

The peak of migration takes place in April and May, when they start to darken as pigmentation takes place. At this stage they are known as elvers, young eels, and are bent on travelling upstream, using tidal currents to migrate to find a river, a lake, a canal, a pond, a body of water that is theirs. They are patiently waiting for the right tide to take them to their water. How do they recognise their own water? They smell it. Elvers have an incredible sense of smell, a forensic ability to smell the traces of passage left in their DNA by their elders.

They are often forced to climb up and out of water as they travel higher and higher. As the elvers migrate their skin thickens, and at the end of the migration, they will be yellow teenaged eels. They also get to choose their sex. This is determined by a number of environmental factors. Those that stay in estuaries and near the sea, or find themselves in high-population densities, become male. Those that pioneer further upstream are female.

If the conditions are hostile, it is best to return to the sea quickly: survival is more likely as a male. But if the conditions are good, it makes sense to be female, even if that means staying longer to develop: the prize of returning to the spawning ground means that an eel's genetic heritage will be passed on as eggs.

They live at the bottom of a number of water bodies, rivers are their natural habitat, but they will thrive in lakes, canals, even large ponds. Here they will mature into silver eels. A mature eel is said to live up to a hundred years, and they regularly reach at least forty, waiting for their great departure back to the Sargasso Sea.

They favour dark, muddy waters with plenty of silt at the bottom to hide in. They nearly always hunt at night, with powerful jaws that are capable of consuming small mammals, fish and invertebrates. They love rotting carrion, hence the horse's head in Gunter Grass's *Tin Drum*.

At some point when the mature silver eel reaches between eight and eighteen years old, it will start to make its way back across the Atlantic to spawn in the warm water of the Sargasso Sea. A mature freshwater eel ready to breed has a dark, grey-brown-black body, and its yellowish sides turn silver and the belly turns silvery white. Their eyes grow much larger and their scales are barely perceptible. They start to store fat. Large eyes allow them to see in the dark depths of ocean waters, the fat reserves fuel their journey, and their pectoral fins lengthen for open-ocean swimming.

No one has witnessed a mature eel spawn in the Sargasso Sea. We know they go home on one of the longest marine migrations, ending in sex and death. Once they return home, all eels die. Eggs are laid, leptocephali hatch and they turn to make the return journey, floating with the marine snow across the ocean.

The mature eels' return journey home has always been a bit of a scientific mystery. It is known that they can migrate here on the warm ocean currents of the Gulf Stream, but how they managed the 5,000 km back seemed impossible. Especially when you learn that on their migration their anus closes and the anal tract atrophies. These are now large fish, easily around fifty centimetres long, tasty fish (though strangely their blood is poisonous to mammals) and 5,000 km is a long way to go without eating. You can't eat if you have no anus.

In 2006, a team of scientists attached very tiny satellites to twenty-two large, mature eels and released them from the coast of Galway. First, they found out that eels don't take a direct route home. Instead of moving in a straight line from Ireland to the Sargasso Sea, they head south to the Azores. This makes sense because there a current will make the migration much easier. It's known that eels swim far too slowly to get to the Sargasso Sea in time for spawning in spring, as they set off from Europe in late summer.

Thus, eels must possess navigational abilities: they don't take the shortest route but the most efficient one, using the subtropical gyre system, a circulating ocean current, that flows to the Caribbean. They do a rather extraordinary dance through the water. During the night the eels swim in shallow, warmer waters; at dawn they descend in a steep dive to 1,000 metres and much cooler waters. It is thought this might delay the final onset of sexual development because at this stage these eels are still teenagers. Their eyes grow bigger because they are entering the abyssal zone in the ocean, where there is no daylight.

How do they know when to go home? Why do they decide to leave on a moonlit night? How do they know where home is?

And how on earth do they make the return journey without eating?

Eels are economical: they fatten up, then fast. No other fish is capable of such frugality. It is thought that the anus may close because, on the long ocean voyage, the eel is less prone to infection, to parasites entering its system; it may be an advantage conferred by evolution. It may also be that the eels are migrating on a cool slipstream almost in hibernation, warming up at night, keeping clear of predators, then using their limited energy to dive down and be pulled by the gyre towards home.

The eel is a prehistoric animal that evolved 70 million years ago and has changed very little since. The Atlantic Ocean appeared 65 million years ago, as a very small ocean. An eel migrating then had an easier journey from the Sargasso Sea to a European river. Since then the ocean has continued to grow: what was once a stroll is now a marathon. Yet still they do it.

What's more, the eel's journey is becoming more difficult. Until very recently eels were considered critically endangered: their European populations had decreased by around 80 per cent and it was thought that by 2020 they might be extinct. One reason for their decline is perhaps the shift in the Gulf Stream, which may be knocking the larvae away from their route. Also, man-made structures are stopping young glass eels getting to their waters. And many more barriers and hydro projects are planned.

Another issue is the parasitic nematode that has spread from Asia to Europe. This pernicious parasite infects the swim bladder, the eel's buoyancy aid, causing lesions and slowing it down, affecting its ability to return to its spawning ground.

However, in the last few years numbers have increased again. In part, this is because there are more eel passages, with the installation of fish ladders, and fewer eels have been caught by fishing. Scientists think, though, that the change in the North Atlantic oscillation index, increasing temperatures between the

North Pole and the Tropic of Cancer, may be sending young eels in the right direction again. Climate change may be operating in the eels' favour.

Still, they remain endangered. For millennia they have survived changing gyres and epic journeys, but humans are altering their habitat. They are fascinating yet vulnerable creatures whose story is still not understood and I hope it may never be. I like to think of them at the bottom of my canals, strange things from far away, prowling the mud below.

* * *

The journey floated past, with autumn's cinematic backdrop of fading leaves, to Dave's deep voice telling one of the best stories I've heard in a long time. By the end, I was completely in love with the slippery eel.

For the final mile or so, we discussed our own lives. We talked about growing older, deciding not to have kids, how to choose happiness and what it looked like. I have watched him grow happier and happier with Louise, and we talked about finally understanding who you are and whom you should be with, the ease and delight in which a good relationship unfolds.

This was the Dave I loved best, the sweet, sensitive, clever man, who has insight, wisdom – and wins all the pub quizzes.

24

The end of September was washed away with autumn rain. The worm-ruined apples rotted on the tree and the garden had a delicious cider perfume. The lank growth of summer's end flopped, and the slugs got back into the business of munching the garden into compost. More boxes, more packing, more change.

In a bid to keep sane, or just to keep going, I packed my boat into the bike bag and headed off to London. I was supposed to be going to an opening night for a design company for Fashion Week, and it was raining hard. I had on a mac, a pair of heels and a short dress while dragging a bike and a bag with paddles sticking out of it. On the train a smartly dressed middle-aged man asked me where I intended to paddle my bike while he stared at my legs. I pointed out there was a boat in the bag and that I was going to paddle on the canals in London. He told me he was supposed to be sea-kayaking in Cornwall at the weekend. I asked him about his trip but it was pretty clear he didn't know much about kayaking, boats, tides or paddles, and I stared him down until he went back to looking at my legs. The male gaze can feel pretty pathetic when it doesn't matter. He mumbled something about not knowing much about boats and stared out of the window.

I was thrown by this, though, as I am every time a man tries to flirt with me or makes an assumption. For the first time I longed for something I could burnish like a badge. I got off the train furious with that man, while recognising that that was a little ridiculous. Then I cycled around in a downpour looking for Charlotte.

We ended up missing the opening and drank in a pub in Liverpool Street. I played out yet another round of the why-did-it-take-me-so-long-to-get-here conversation. In it I looked for legitimacy while another part of me cornered the questioner and shouted, 'What do you expect to get from this question?'

It plagued me over and over again. Had I been lying to myself all that time? Did I not know myself? Was I ignorant or scared or just plain stupid? In a world where we're asked to make bold, assured statements about ourselves, admitting halfway through that I'd been on the wrong track was a mighty strange thing. Though I believe wholly that negative capability is essential, that everyone is capable of inhabiting uncertainty, it is an extremely uncomfortable place at times. The truth is that I don't know why it took me so long. I know that I was loved and loved back, so if it wasn't exactly right, it didn't seem wrong to remain married. I know that I might one day understand and that, by embracing all the uncertainty, making peace with the ambiguity of my situation will be my reward one day for asking the question.

As Rainer Maria Rilke wrote in *Letters to a Young Poet*, 'I beg you to have patience with everything unresolved in your heart and to try to love the questions themselves as if they were locked rooms or books written in a foreign language. Don't search for answers which could not be given to you now, because you would not be able to live them. And the point is to live everything. Live the questions now. Perhaps then, someday far in the future, you will gradually, without even noticing it, live your way to the answers.'

*   *   *

I left London the following morning. I was in waterproof boots and jeans, and ten minutes after I'd arrived in Moor Street I was on the water, paddling home.

Autumn had started delicately to touch everything. I noticed fat alder cones ripening and, on the banks, puffballs bursting forth – they looked both dangerous and enticing. The broadleaf plantains that lined the far side of the canal grew majestically in the short grass with no mower to hold them back. Their batons for seed heads swayed just above me, and seen from below in the boat, they were resplendent. They looked as if they owned their spot and could own a spot in a garden. I paddled over to look at them closely, those common lawn weeds.

Cotoneaster grows everywhere along the canals. Bird-distributed seed sprouts wherever it can, caring little whether the soil is poor or rich. It may be a pedestrian plant, but its flowers are a great source of nectar and pollen to insects and its berries will keep many birds fed in early winter. In the morning sun, they looked like embers burning against the dark-green foliage. I paddled slowly on. I'd done a little of this journey before and I hesitated at a turning, wondering whether to explore another section, but decided that after weeks of frenetic travelling, going homeward would be most rewarding. I headed back towards Digbeth.

I'd forgotten there were so many locks with tiny bridge passages and ended up slinging the boat on my back and pushing the bike for half a mile or so. A passing runner offered to help as I wobbled along, like some strange ninja turtle with a bright-red shell. I felt frustrated by my lack of planning and wondered whether I should turn back and find the unexplored parts. I lingered on a bank trying to decide, watching the bulrushes sway in a side pond. I decided I was tired and hungry. I walked through the Curzon Street tunnel, passing two narrowboats, and launched back into the water. I paddled over to Typhoo Basin to see if the homeless man was still there with his marvellous shack. Either he'd been found out or he'd moved on. There was nothing to speak of his presence, except the black soot of his fire up one wall and a small framed picture that said 'Imagine that . . . ? Live like that . . . ?' Then there was a Superman-style diamond with a G in the middle and 'KHATERA SUPER BOHATERA! W.K.' It was tied up with blue twine and the bottom of the frame was missing.

No one would see that strange outsider art because it was behind the metal barriers that stopped people using the towpath into the basin. I sat staring at it for some time, trying to find meaning in it. Now that the space was empty, it seemed small. It was hard to imagine three rooms under that bridge.

The basin seemed dull without his presence, exposed and less magical. I paddled over to see if I could spot some pike in the sun as I drank soup from a flask Charlotte had packed me off with that morning. After the soup, which was full of ginger and chilli, with the sun on the red bricks and more cotoneaster berries burning away, I was suddenly exhausted and uninterested in pike spotting. I tied up the boat to a buddleja, slung my feet over the side and fell asleep, the sun acting as a blanket.

I woke fifteen minutes later, drifting, untied from my buddleja mooring, and felt cold, the way outdoor autumn naps leave you. I paddled out of the basin and round the corner. I dipped into the disused factory-side pool to see if I could spot the heron and, with no luck, paddled on down towards Digbeth.

Floating autumnal leaves were a surprising treat: they swirled around, hurling and furling themselves onto the water and the boat. The air smelt of ripening apples and of other years. I floated past the huge fig that had turned into a thicket, a forest if you were small enough, rather than a single tree. All the ripe figs were high above and there was no way of reaching them, so I flitted in and out of the leaves and their dappled shade enjoying the great tangle of branches. A little further on I sampled a few blackberries and came upon a feral apple tree that had prostrated itself on the bank and grew exactly as the wild apples I had seen in Kazakhstan, along the banks of the high alpine rivers.

The apple clearly had some Braeburn parentage, but was tasty and I took a few for the journey. Clever apple. It might have looked like a straggle of a tree, but the apples would fall into the water and float. It's clear when you visit wild apple forests that apples do very well next to rivers. The fruit is buoyant, and I found a number of trees by following bobbing apples back upstream to the parent. I liked the thought of the world's most boring apple, the Braeburn, realising some of its wildling genes in inner-city Birmingham.

Around this point an older man on a bike stopped and gestured for me to paddle over. Wary for no good reason, other than that he wasn't clear about what he wanted, I stopped and stared, waiting for clarity. He asked if I was married and why I was in a boat. I felt no need to answer either question so I paddled on. He followed on his bike and shouted that I should get out and have sex with him. It was such a ludicrous suggestion that I laughed, and then he followed me for half a mile or so. I wondered what on earth possessed him to think he'd win this one. I sat in the middle of the canal with the boat twirling round, head to one side staring at him, until eventually he left.

Three youths looked on as they smoked weed on a bridge against a brilliant backdrop of graffiti that resembled a Klee painting. I felt irritated and perhaps a little bored by them so I turned a corner and paddled up a safe distance to get out unwatched. I folded the boat, assembled the bike and cycled off in the opposite direction. I pushed the bike over a steep bridge crossing the canal, and saw, in a corner, a forlorn squab, a baby pigeon, naked and abandoned. It must have fallen from its nest. Pigeons produce something called pigeon milk from the lining of the crop that they regurgitate to the young. They usually raise only two birds because they are limited by how much milk they produce. It is more like cottage cheese than milk but is high in protein and fat. The squab looked older than a week, so it was now used to eating adult food, but it was too young to survive. Squabs are punkish-looking and not pretty. It was hopeless, and I felt hopeless about it.

*　　*　　*

Pidgey and Softboy is the name of a comic book that H and I loved. Softboy is a sort of dumpy cuddly toy who desperately wants to be friends with Pidgey, the pigeon. Every attempt at cultivating this friendship ends with Pidgey taking startled flight, as pigeons do. That upright takeoff leaves Softboy heartbroken and confused, but not perhaps as confused as Pidgey: why would a toy want to cuddle him? This was one of the many comics I lost when I left my marriage. I say lost, but it wasn't mine to keep, just part of a past library. Like remembering a certain sentence is on the right or the left page, roughly how far into a book you were, or how the spine of a certain book looks, it's just another thing to try to recall.

Pigeons, also known more romantically as rock doves, *Columba livia*, take flight in that startled manner not because they are necessarily alarmed or even surprised but because they evolved around rocks, talus at the foot of cliffs, rock faces and outcrops. Their ancestors would have nested on ledges so they would have had to develop a wing structure that allowed them to take off at a sharp, steep angle, perhaps into strong winds. Their wing arc can be raised up to 180 degrees, an angle that allows them extraordinary power. On top of that they evolved out of rock outcrops with turbulent wind patterns, so when gliding they can create a very steep dihedral angle – the angle between the bird's wing and true horizontal, making the bird very stable even in windy conditions.

When you read about pigeons, a certain tone prevails. It is nearly always a little derogatory, a little surprised that they might have a habitat or habit that should be noticed. Pigeons are too often seen as stupid, too ubiquitous to be interesting, too happy in pollution to be admired, too feral, too able to survive. What other bird do you see so often disabled?

In the book, *The Breeding Birds of the London Area*, we discover that 'Almost every square or open space, however, provides a feeding ground for some pigeons, and smaller numbers, which probably total many hundreds, if not thousands, forage in the gutters of the quieter streets for their living.' To many, they are flying rats, vermin that roost in nooks and crannies and fill the air with the acrid smell of their guano.

They are known to eat the mortar from buildings and thought to cause considerable damage, though in reality their beaks are not strong enough for that; they mainly eat crumbling mortar from weak buildings. They do this because they originated in rocky limestone areas and need considerable amounts of lime to lay eggs.

The pigeon was domesticated by early man, partly because their relationship was commensal, which means a relationship in which one organism derives a large benefit (the pigeon) and the other derives neither benefit nor harm (the human). You will often see pigeons in flocks around humans, eating our crumbs – they are very good at availing themselves of surplus human food. Some might have been taken by early humans to caves and decided sensibly to stay and make the most of food caches. Or they might have found their way to messy human caves and stayed to eat the food detritus. Eventually we started eating pigeon and became their predators, but when we stopped being nomadic and became farmers we developed an appreciation for pigeon guano: it is rich in nitrogen so we domesticated the rock dove.

The feral pigeon, the city dove, is derived from the domesticated pigeon but returned to the wild (or the street). Whether truly wild, domesticated or feral, they are now all considered the same species, *Columbia livia domestica*, as happy on sea cliffs as it is on mountain outcrops or building ledges.

They are a ubiquitous species, and are synanthropic, meaning they live near and benefit from an association with humans, often in somewhat artificial habitats that we have created. If you look at a feral pigeon in horror and declare it a 'rat with wings', then you have helped to create a world in which it can be so.

25

October would be our last autumn adventure. The water was so cool now that it meant paddling was limited by freezing fingers. I'd almost covered the map, so the mission was drawing to a close.

I messaged Ming and Sarah. We debated various routes. We were off the map now, heading out to the Black Country again, this time to Walsall via Tipton. Tipton is not a place you might readily choose to go to. It looks as if it got stuck in the seventies. The shops have brown plastic lettering above the window or door. There's a hairdresser, a chippy, a cheap booze outlet and a betting shop. It is poor. It has a lot of English Defence League and gang-related graffiti. We saw a number of shrines for young men killed along the canal. The first towpath users to engage us were a group of young men who'd 'just bought a motorbike for eight pounds' and were off to joy-ride it. They turned out to be among a number of young men riding motorbikes too fast, on too narrow a strip, the machines often fuelled on chip fat so that the engines banged and farted with the effort to keep going. The majority of other towpath users walked fighting dogs. There was a lot of crazy-person graffiti about God, angry graffiti about politics, deranged graffiti about superpowers, and too much memorial graffiti. We wondered how all those young men had died – in fights, falling off bikes into the canals, being shot or stabbed?

The canal felt safe, even if the margins seemed dodgy. And it had its hidden nature, its surprising delights, and by the end I'd become someone who'd choose to go to Tipton again.

Once Tipton was the Black Country's most heavily industrialised area, with thousands of people employed in its many industries. Tipton, not Birmingham, was known as the 'Venice of the Midlands' for its extensive canal network. In 1800, four thousand people were living in an area originally settled for its farmland; by the end of the century, thirty thousand lived in an area dominated by factory chimneys billowing polluted black smoke onto the houses built cheek by jowl beside them. By the 1970s nearly all of the industry had died out and the early-nineteenth-century houses had been demolished. It still has its watery industrial backbone running through it, with some elegant bridges and a few factories, but mostly the Venice of the Midlands is a ghostly, forgotten place.

Sarah and Ming picked me up from the local railway station and we drove around in circles in a commuter housing estate, trying to locate the canal. New builds always feel like film sets, the picture-perfect houses with shiny front doors and weed-free driveways. In Ming and Sarah's campervan, we must have looked like hippie stoners. We located the canal up a surprisingly rural footpath with a five-bar wooden gate. It was framed by a small thicket of trees on either side that made a tunnel to pass through. Up on the canal – around there you are nearly always rising above or slicing through the landscape because these are late-century canals, poker straight to drive business to business – the rural idyll disappeared. The water was rubbish strewn and there was a slight wind blowing towards us.

I launched my boat and headed off. Someone had been verge-cutting so the edges were torn and battered. The sky was the colour of potter's clay and smeared the water into a thin sheet of grey. Almost immediately we ran into the boys with the stolen motorbike, though Sarah had to point this out to me – naively, I had commented that eight pounds was very cheap for a bike. Had I been alone, this could have made for a bleak, unnerving setting, but none of that mattered because I was with friends and the boats. The adventure was ours for the seizing.

We hadn't seen each other for a while and for the first bit of the journey we caught up on news. They were tired because they had been binge-watching box sets they'd learnt recently how to download. We discussed the merits of various shows, which characters we'd be in *Orange Is the New Black* and whom we'd sleep with. Silly conversations that had me giggling until the boat spun in circles. Having frivolous conversations felt dizzyingly delightful, like thin air at the top of a mountain. I was lost outside my preoccupations.

We travelled under various bridges, met various towpath users, lonely anglers smoking Woodbines, angry men, young men, boys with their granddads learning to fish, a couple pushing a pram with a Staffie. The water was litter-strewn all the way, mostly with beer cans and bottles. We passed a small industrial unit that was belching out the scent of washing powder in great plumes of white air. It was strange to smell cleanliness and order in an environment that was quite the opposite.

We came to the first pretty bit, a small fringe of arrowroot and bulrushes, with a family of swans, the parents and three gangly overgrown teenagers, yet to shed their childish feathers. The father was fierce and angry, wings up. He split the family so it was clear which way we should pass. I hung to the side and Ming and Sarah led out to the left, suddenly chasing the family over to me. I had a sudden panic as I realised I was drifting closer to the cob rather than away. I paddled hard and lowered my gaze, while he honked at our departure, clearly unable to make sense of what the strange floating things were.

A little way on we spotted a grey heron sitting on a power line. He took off when he spotted us, then slowly circled us. I had never seen such behaviour in a heron. Clearly it was waiting to land and our lingering meant that it looked like a plane in a holding pattern, wasting fuel until it could land. Herons are strange birds on the ground, those long thin legs, that razor-sharp beak, the long bendy neck and those somewhat dishevelled feathers. It's hard to imagine them as graceful in the sky, but up there they tuck themselves in, retracting the long neck so that it nestles in the wings, trailing their long legs together so that they look like a tail on a kite. As it slowly circled, I thought it looked remarkably human, like Icarus falling from the sky, those large wings with tips outstretched.

We stayed still, gazing at the bird, until we started to drift. Watching wildlife do something you haven't witnessed before is compulsive viewing, but they are probably behaving in that unusual way simply because you're there, in the way, unnerving them. You choose to come and look at them, but they don't choose to look at you. It was time to move on.

We had done several miles very fast, and stopped to drink coffee and eat snacks. I offered flapjacks, which I'd made in a bid to feel settled when I arrived back from London. I'd produced a mountain of them, a whole tray to use up some bananas, and had ended up eating them for breakfast, lunch and supper, with no one to feed any more. H rarely wanted to eat anything I cooked now and was often out in the evenings.

The land around where we were was scrub and a vast electrical power station hummed and buzzed. It was no place to linger, and because of that the margins were pretty. We found some council strimmers under a bridge, flooding their motors after pulling too hard on the string. Grass clippings littered the canal all the way up, but here the grass was short, the soil clearly calcareous, and everything was a little stunted. Along the edges there was a fringe of blue fleabane, *Erigeron acer*, not uncommon but fairly picky about where it sits so it was a find, for me at least. The towpath sat high above the boat so I could look up at the sky through a lace of fleabane. The greyness and the threat of rain had passed and now white fluffy clouds raced over a beautiful blue. The fleabane is a funny little thing: the species name, *acer*, refers to its bitter taste and it was once used for toothache. It's not pretty but there is something charming about it, or charming at any rate in its strange electrical setting. It has tiny reduced-ray florets that are somewhere between lilac pink and blue-white, and a rather swollen receptacle beneath.

The buzz of the power station was a little sickening and we decided to move on promptly. The final straight stretch was an easy paddle, a few bridges with more cryptic graffiti, a factory that smelt of curry powder and crisps, and scrubland.

We hit a junction on the canal and decided to push on for a bit longer. To the left was a very pretty bridge, Hempole Bridge, with a single elliptical arch and sandstone coping, and a cast-iron plate, stating '1825'. Its walls were curved and elegant. The bridge to the right was not nearly so pretty and thus the decision was made. Two small schoolboys standing on the bridge above us took bets on which of us would race ahead.

On the other side of Hempole Bridge was a disused double railway bridge, one for each line, no longer in use, with trees sprouting where they could. One of the bridges had fine iron detailing, the other was a thicket of wild plants. The water widened and bulrushes and reed sweet-grass rubbed shoulders with willow.

The sun was just peeking out. It wasn't exactly an idyll, but it was a far cry from the black-and-white photos of the area taken at some point post-war that I'd found on the internet. They showed a bleak industrial setting, with no trees, huge chimney stacks that billowed something acrid enough to be evident in a poorly exposed picture. The railway line was clearly in use, and almost nothing was growing other than a little fringe of grass. After fifty years of industrial decline and no railway, we found huge ceps growing in hazel and birch thickets. Fifty years of neglect had also given rise to that English Defence League graffiti and all those men walking fighting dogs. Fifty years on, wild things owned the railway tracks. We watched a rat leap into the water, swim deftly across the canal and leap out the other side, run up the bridge abutments under the arch and onto the deck. It did this with such grace and ease that it was hard not to be impressed. In fact, we wished aloud it had been a water vole so that we could like it.

It started to spit with rain and we turned to head back to our pick-up location. I asked Sarah where she'd left the car, and she replied, 'Near Charlotte's bridge. I thought it was appropriate.'

We got out to pink skies as the sun set behind us. The rain hadn't settled in. The canal was still littered with beer cans, the verge cutting had done little to improve the path and another stolen motorbike roared past. Charlotte's name was graffitied on the far side of the bridge in yellow spray paint.

I'd see her the next evening. I'd take my beloved dog to my mother's house in the countryside for a little respite from her broken home and get back on another train, to watch the countryside whistle past until I hit London and ran the last bit to Charlotte's front door, leaping over the tree roots that blistered the pavement tarmac, running my fingers through the ribbon of ivy that grew out of the neighbour's front garden, stopping just before the ash outside her house and listening.

Not knocking, just listening to her footsteps on the floorboards, to her opening cupboards and calling the cat. I listened in the cold October air to the sounds of her home, of her at home. 'Home,' I said aloud, trying the word, and then I pulled out the key. She opened the door before I could turn the lock.

26

'I think my spirit animal might be a rat,' I told Charlotte, on a walk in Scotland. She was quiet, contemplative and didn't want to think about spirit animals. I prodded a little. Perhaps there was a fish she'd like to be? A brightly coloured one that no one eats, apparently. 'Perhaps you'd get fished out of your home for a pet-supply shop, like all those clown fish, and be tormented by a small child,' I suggested.

'I won't be one of those,' she replied.

The spirit-animal conversation was going no further.

I think my spirit animal is a rat because I have had a number of close-up and personal experiences with rats. I haven't liked any of them. I don't want to repeat them, but they have left me curious as to how I and those rats ended up in such close quarters.

I had my first rat experience when I was very young. A rat got trapped in a grain bin in the chicken shed. When I opened the lid it jumped out. Now that wasn't surprising, but with a large grain bin, you tend to open the lid with one hand and dip in a scoop with the other so that the bin contents are shrouded in darkness. Thus the first part of my scoop was filled not with corn but the uneven weight of a furry thing. It was too heavy for me to support so it used my arm in its bid for freedom. A rat running up your arm is pretty terrifying. I have subsequently met many a jumping rat, mostly from compost bins, but that was my first.

My second significant rat experience was in New York when I was nineteen – actually, there were two experiences. In the first, I was walking down East 6th Street, in what must have been my first or second week when I heard lots of squeaking coming out of a dustbin. Now you'd think my first experience all those years back would have taught me not to open bins carelessly, but memories fade. At that point I thought all New Yorkers were difficult, because they queue-jumped, shouted at each other and seemed to relish being rude. They were the sort, of course, who might trap kittens in a bin. I was going to release those poor kittens and save them from the rude New Yorkers. They weren't kittens. The bin was full of the largest rats I have ever seen and they poured out. I have no idea what had been going on in that bin – a rat orgy, a feast of huge proportions, or a trick. I slammed down the lid and danced among scattering rats, swearing like a true New Yorker.

My second New York rat was in a subway and was dead. I stared at it for a long time because I could see it was dead but I could also see its mouth moving. I wondered if I was going mad, if that crazy city was driving me over the edge. Then, as my focus took hold, I realised its mouth was moving because it was exploding with maggots. I threw up just as the train pulled in.

My final significant rat experience was when I got bitten by one that had taken residence in my chicken house. It's a good story. The rat and I fought, battled, even. It would not let go of me. I ended up thumping my hand against a tree to force it to release its jaws. There was spurting blood, a visit to A and E, an orderly who sang UB40's 'Rat In Mi Kitchen', a needle, a syringe so large I still wince thinking about it, and a course of antibiotics that made me woozy for weeks.

That final experience led me to examine why I kept running into rats and, in part, the answer is simple: because I'm human.

*   *   *

I did not see as many rats as I imagined I might on the canals, but I knew that many rats ran there and the few that I did see were magnificent creatures, fine examples of how a rat can be.

The swimming rat that Ming, Sarah and I saw was athletic and made a sequence of moves a James Bond stunt coordinator would have been proud of. It was brave and balletic; it was unashamed. It was not running away from us, just going somewhere else. When I see a rat behave like that, I think, Those are good spirit-animal attributes.

I once saw a rat picking a fight with a squirrel. It went on for days in my neighbour's garden when the snow lay so thick that anything outdoors had to forgo being shy. Every day the squirrel and the rat would fight over the bird food. We couldn't get to the allotment or the pub so the squirrel-versus-rat saga took over our lives. Riveted, we watched round after round, keeping tally, taking bets. A blackbird joined in one day, like a Johnny-come-lately in a pub brawl, but dashed away when it realised the stakes were too high. I kept it quiet that I was on the rat's side.

Even my lover, who tolerates a lot from me, wasn't that impressed by my rat spirit-animal confession. If you google 'rat' as your animal spirit you get a lot of predictable notions, mostly that you are adaptable, resourceful, willing to change, a survivor. And apparently you like to hoard stuff, particularly when times are tough and you feel insecure. I think of my jam cupboard. I guess no one wants to point out you've chosen the most invasive species on the planet as your talismanic beast.

It is likely that rats came either from woodlands and forests or from cliff faces. They are among that wider group of pigeons, mice, wolves (and thus dogs) and wildcats (and thus domestic cats) that probably evolved alongside humans in caves on rocky places, cliffs, outcrops and other such low-elevation landscapes, part of the talus ecology that is so akin to city life. Those rocky cliff faces are the high rises and concrete-scapes of our towns and cities.

27

A glorious warm autumn ended in a wet thud, and the winds whipped the garden into chaos. Charlotte and I watched fireworks in drizzle in a country park, then walked back along the beaches of Margate to bed. I had been avoiding home. I carried on my back what I needed to get by. Stripped of worldly possessions, when I did go home I marvelled that I had ever accumulated so much stuff.

I ran my finger along shelves where books were missing. H had still not found somewhere to live and the house was littered with two lives in limbo. Our married life was being packed away for ever. There were endless boxes of stuff for H's new life, a new tea caddy, spoons, a bread bin. I say new, but they weren't: he was mostly duplicating our old life together. The same vintage stuff, old but new to him. I found it deeply upsetting. I kept offering him our old stuff, but he continued to buy identical replacements.

I looked around the rooms and realised how cluttered the house had become, how with less stuff it would be easier. I looked at mantelpieces and knew that none of the things that sat on them would stay with me – so too with the paintings on the walls, the knick-knacks, the carpets, the TV, the stereo. I'd be left with books, houseplants and the sofa neither of us liked. I didn't feel bereft for the stuff I would lose. I didn't want to replace like for like. I didn't even know if I cared for any of it any more. I felt a pang, though, when I looked at the garden, which was still unravelling into a wild space. But then again I rather liked that wild space. The blackbird that had eaten all the blueberries was back for the grapes and apples I hadn't harvested. A ripe tomato, fallen to the ground, was cracked and blackened, slowly rotting back to where it had come from. The path had disappeared – the garden was lush and overgrown and hidden. The wildlife loved it: undisturbed, they were throwing its contents around. The rotting and half dying were piling up into an extraordinary feast.

I sent our beloved dog to live with my parents while the house was dismantled. H was saddened and angry that I would do this. She wore her heart on her sleeve and was tortured by our separation, running from one of us to the other, pawing at us, slowly growing thinner. Her absence at home was painful, when I was there. I dreamt of her endlessly, mostly walking her, often along canals, although we'd never done that. Her absence also meant this was coming to an end. It was over. H and I would never be together again. I felt relieved, and terrified by my relief. It all came back to the same fear: if I had done this for so long, for fourteen years, how could I trust myself again? I was paralysed at times by the thought that I had deceived myself.

This led to a crippling lack of confidence. I flustered my way through talks for work. I wavered over words on the page, forgot the names of plants, and for a week I convinced myself I'd forgotten how to kiss. I would look back on the previous day and be awestruck that I'd got through it. The future was blinding. I longed to daydream again, but I couldn't find any tales to get lost in other than my own self-centred version.

I traced back over the map. The canals I had fallen in love with, the stretches I had gone back over, like the Icknield Loop and around Digbeth, had become familiar: I knew them as you do shortcuts. They were mine now because I had created stories there. I found out that the Icknield Loop was to have 6,000 houses built around it. My city was changing and so would my canals.

The deep boom of the factories, the hideaways, the old rotting hulls that acted as ponds, the forest of birch and alder seen through misty mornings, the mushrooms, the berries, the litter, the broken glass, the pathways made by foxes, the pigeons' nests and the rats' burrows. Within the next five years they would all be gone.

A new generation would grow up with the Cut as part of their green landscape, their ecology. This new development boasted that you'd be able to walk, run or ride to town without ever having to cross a road or meet a car. There was even talk that the reservoir might be opened for swimming. The water quality is superb and it would cost less to run than a new swimming-pool. The unsettled landscape would change once again. Those that had temporarily called it home would go somewhere else. Some would stay – the fish might not even notice what was happening. Some would be given better provision – the herons, kingfishers and water voles would be held up as shining examples of nature in the city, a reason to move there. The rats wouldn't be tolerated: their temporary respite from being hunted would end. The mushrooms might reappear – someone might even start picking them. New people would take up fishing, some child would be bird watching and others would learn to conquer the toll islands. Someone would lose their beloved cat to the Cut. Others might learn to swim there – and buy inflatable boats to paddle around. The Cut might endure another dirty, forgotten stage, but between now and then, there would be a clean-up. It would become gentrified or sterilised, depending on how you see these things.

28

I went to London and took my boat with me. Autumn was retiring. Soon it would be too cold for paddling. I spent so much time, sometimes joyously, sometimes frustrated, in London that it seemed only right that one of my final paddles should be there. I'd spent much of the summer writing in Charlotte's studio that looked down over the canal. I wrote to the honk of geese, to the purr of canal-boat engines, to the incessant bells of cyclists on the towpath. It was now time I tried paddling it.

I strained my foot, I didn't know how. It was one of a series of injuries where my mind quietly failed me. I had taken to walking into things and waking up with new bruises in places that made no sense. My mind and my body were still slightly separated and my body failed to remind me of this. My concentration was elsewhere. My body tripped me up to slow me down. I hobbled about London's streets unable to put my heel down. As I couldn't march, I decided I should float instead. My heel was grateful for that, my hands less so.

The water was cold. Kayaking means that you're constantly dripped on by the paddle. It doesn't matter how good your technique is, you'll always get wet. I should have ordered the boat with a spray deck, a thin waterproof cover to keep the paddle water off your legs, but I didn't know of that hazard. On warm days a gentle sprinkling of canal water was neither here nor there, but on cool ones wet hands, wet cuffs and wet legs are exhausting. I took my scarf off and used it as a blanket to keep my legs warm, if not dry.

Before I got into the water I had breakfast. After the years I'd spent being so parsimonious about money, London opened my purse and scattered the contents everywhere. For the first time in my life I equated being outside with losing money. Every step seemed to end in some sort of purchase. I bought beetroot instead of growing it. It felt so strange to pick up something rather than pull it out of the ground. I smarted at having to pay for breakfast but I also knew I couldn't paddle for hours on an empty stomach. I ordered the cheapest thing, sourdough bread and avocado. The chef mistook my order and I ended up with feta cheese, a poached egg and some avocado all beautifully arranged in a box. I took it and my black coffee down to the canal and started to unwrap the boat.

A young woman in tiny black denim shorts, thick black tights and a slick of black eye-liner walked past with several highly strung dogs. Her oversized fleece, which she clearly didn't much care for, said she was a dog-walker. We both looked down at my boat and probably thought the same thing: the fringe of grass it sat on was green for one reason alone. This was Dog Piss Alley. I smiled at her and wedged my coffee and box of breakfast in the crook of a branch of the only tree around, a weedy, battle-torn sycamore with a huge scar in its trunk.

Several personal trainers dragged along their clients, like the young woman was dragging the dogs, and a number of too-fast, too-aggressive cyclists fired their bells at me. There was not enough space on that towpath. I tried to shuffle my stuff in a bit more and continued to blow up the boat. There was little wind and it was a slow process. I felt self-conscious, as if I was another hipster trying to make a playground of that already overused space.

The canal was much lower than the path. I realised I'd have to launch myself, my breakfast and all of my gear in one swift move if I was not to lose everything. I tied the boat to my belt loop, put the coffee on the edge and threw my gear and the breakfast into the prow. Then I leapt in. I knew the boat well enough that I could stand upright for a few seconds. I grabbed the paddle as I lowered myself, then used it to steady myself to the side and grabbed the coffee. There was a strong wind and undercurrent and the boat slid off into a slipstream without a stroke from me.

A well-dressed mother with a pram pointed me out to her child. 'Look, darling, there's a woman in a dinghy, drinking coffee.' They both waved at me. I was a Hackney parody.

I drank my coffee as two geese honked overhead. Canada geese, *Branta canadensis*, that live in the UK don't migrate: they got here and decided to call it home. Like many of the Anatidae family, swans, ducks and other geese, Canada geese mate for life. They actively mourn the loss of a partner and are attentive parents. Canada geese were introduced in the late seventeenth century to James II's waterfowl collection in St James's Park and have hung around ever since. The number of birds was relatively low till the 1950s, when a bunch of enthusiasts, rather strangely helped on by the Wildfowl Trust, decided to distribute breeding pairs around the country.

These birds are not just faithful to their partners but to home: they nearly always stay close to where they hatched, eating aquatic and terrestrial plants and waiting, if necessary, for breeding territory to become available. It makes sense that when all they did was hang around St James's Park they remained a small number. Grazing rights would have determined population growth. Take breeding pairs and distribute them left, right and centre, though, and you'll have a baby boom. With little predation, a happy couple can easily raise four or five young per year, and if there's enough grass to eat, happy families grow quickly. Canada geese became ubiquitous in the British Isles to the unfortunate point of being considered a pest.

Urban areas suit them best, with plenty of green grass in parks to eat, few predators, other than the odd fox, and nesting sites that are inaccessible to all but the occupants. I've seen Canada geese nest happily on the lip of the factory wall by the edge of the canal with no more than a few twigs to mark their home. Both parents are fiercely territorial of their nests. I've eyeballed many a gander, shouting back as loudly as he honked to defend my right to paddle past. Once the young are hatched the parents rightly become more territorial: big mammals, rather than the fox, are their major predator so nobody should be surprised when a goose chases a toddler.

Now I watched the pair above me fly off towards Limehouse and wondered whether they'd just got together or had been doing that for years.

I finished my coffee and set off in the same direction: if the map was right I should be able to paddle into the Thames. That sounded potentially dangerous and thus a perfect adventure because, apart from buddleja, floating duckweed and the occasional coot, there was not a great deal to see where I was.

When I wasn't amid a green soup of duckweed, which is surprisingly hard to paddle through, the water was crystal clear. I could see bedposts, bicycles, tricycles, scooters, toys, beer bottles and cans, lighters, road signs, locks, and all the other things people think will disappear into the depths but don't. The water was clear partly because the weather was getting colder but mostly because there wasn't a great deal of traffic to disturb the mud layer. I soon realised that the majority of the narrowboats on the canal rarely moved. It's not cheap to live on a houseboat in London, but it's a lot cheaper than living on land.

There were Canal and River Trust advertising boards on every available clear edge, trumpeting of future moorings, boasting of electricity, locked gates and other amenities. For great stretches, there were boats at either side, sometimes two deep, so that the water was just wide enough for a narrowboat to pass but little else. I thought of Dave's lovely mooring on the basin in the centre of Birmingham and all those tiny hidden stretches where the trees fringed the sides and no one passed, of the lovely moorings I'd found in the most unlikely areas, in Wednesbury, Tipton, Dudley and Walsall, places where you could turn a corner, the city receded and an unexpected retreat appeared. Here, the boaters were like land-dwellers, locked in and rather cramped. Still, there were plenty of delights, with bars, cafés and nightlife just the other side of the towpath. I could see why narrowboats had become so popular there.

I saw a young angler using winter light gear and lures, a short rod and everything else on his back. He was casting out hopefully, reeling back disappointed, on and on. I said, 'Hi!' but he didn't answer. I'd come to an invisible line that the duckweed refused to cross and peered into the clear water again in the hope of seeing a fish. Even in the murkiest water in Birmingham I'd catch a glimpse of something, if I stayed still, but there I saw nothing. I knew secretly that I wished to see nothing. I wanted Birmingham's canals to have something over London's.

I paddled back into the duckweed soup. A coot followed me. When I turned back I could see the dip, dip, dip of my paddle, crescent-moon turns, as my boat and I waddled through. I passed Victoria Park and more runners. With little plant life to contemplate, I considered Lycra in its various guises and ate my breakfast.

29

We left in winter to go to a remote island in the Hebrides. We left in a flurry of bad weather that we dodged until we couldn't and ended up hydroplaning in the dark through Storm Desmond in my £750 eBay-purchased van. It felt like a great adventure. I didn't stop then to think that more water was rushing through my life as the Yorkshire villages flooded and every bridge we attempt to cross had been washed away. We drove late into the night over the mountains. I gripped the steering wheel and tried not to think about how inexperienced I was as a driver.

Charlotte longs to be able to live in the Hebrides, and I'd always fantasised about writing in a remote location. I'd finish this book there, I thought, away from any distractions. It was a perfect place, windswept and wild. But writing about the joys of feral pigeons, or why pike and nettles are such adaptable natives that they can make themselves at home even in our worst pollution, while the skies outside raced clouds and threw out rainbows, the ground wove a tapestry of husky purple from fading heather, the brilliant burnt umber of bracken and the shocking mossy green of sheep-nibbled grass against the metallic mirror of rain-drenched granite rocks? With the half-light of early morning or the gloom of late afternoon flicking across the landscape, picking out flecks of colour, like a good tweed cloth. With a backdrop of the seas turning from peppermint green to cool blue? Writing was impossible. Why exalt concrete and its ecology of liverworts and mosses when you could walk through birch outcrops dripping tree lungwort, a lichen so large, lush and green that it seems fake, a lichen that can grow only where there is no pollution?

This was a landscape that begged to be observed minute by minute.

I became consumed by it. I suited it in so many ways. I could lie down and become instantly lost. We laughed at how my hair was the same colour as the bracken. If I sat very quietly among the brittle heather even the dog lost me – I could watch her scanning till she picked up my scent on a new breeze.

I had run to the furthest reaches of my country and this land-scape left me yearning for a sense of place. If not here, then where? If not now, then when?

In the true darkness of night, so immense that the stars tumbled all the way to the ground, in a place so remote you could shout to the sea and never be heard, the rain tapped insistently at rattling windows. I lay in bed running through all the places that I thought of as home, all the landscapes that might have been mine. I chased the past in circles, riding my nightmares. I woke in the crack between the two single beds, clinging to either side to stay in place.

And all this time the wind howled, storm after storm passed through the landscape, and in the end I felt there was nothing left to do but join it.

I let winter's wild furies in. I became the weather. Then when the storms had blown out and the furies' sirens were silent, it became too much. Too much sky, too wide a vista, too much landscape ever-changing underfoot. I cracked. I poured out my tension into the seeping bogs and the fissures in the rocks. I blew up the sky and wailed into the waterfalls. I picked over the dead sheep carcasses, wrenched teeth out of the skulls and clenched them in my hands till they left bite marks. I collected bones washed smooth by the sea and examined the liverworts, mosses and lichens for their hidden worlds. I peered endlessly into the recesses of this world, looking for any sort of answer. I started walking alone in the hope of finding solitude and peace, but raged from one side of the island to the other. I dragged the dog through hailstorms and up mountains, but in the end even she couldn't cope with my restlessness.

It is the most beautiful landscape fuelled by real weather, breathtaking, but there is too much space: it's too open, too wild, too relentless for someone questioning everything. I went to find peace to write, the old cliché that every writer believes they need, and I couldn't cope. I can't tell you exactly why I couldn't because I still don't understand it, other than that I got up to the wilds and realised I was deeply unsettled. I needed familiarity. I needed home.

*   *   *

I bordered the ferry wet with tears as the sea lashed around me. Exhausted from little sleep, I drove hard through the Great Glen. I wept with the rain in Ben Nevis and as I wound down through the Cairngorms, traffic snaking behind me, my windscreen weeping as hard as I was. I finally fell exhausted into a warm bed at an empty B-and-B, which was about to close for the season. I drifted off to sleep during a documentary about rock pools and clinging limpets.

In the morning I sped to Glasgow airport on the last of my adrenalin before, broke and exhausted, I handed the van's keys to my friend Clare. She took me to Ming and Sarah's, listening to my broken record: who was I, where was I, where was I going?

*   *   *

Ming and Sarah fed me and the dog, let us both fall asleep on their sofas, distracted us, walked us and didn't mind when I sobbed or the dog barked. I contemplated going paddling, going to the movies, going to meet friends, but in the end I sat on the sofa and consumed cheese and box sets.

Every morning they walked me across Sutton Park, walking my anxiety out of me. Sutton Coldfield: the latter part of its name derives from the medieval charcoal burning that took place in the vast park. It's the seventh largest urban park in Europe. Walk into it and you lose the city quickly – 2,400 acres or so of wetland, ancient wood, Roman roads, five ponds, one restaurant, wild ponies, the odd cow, a wealth of bird life, and dog-walkers.

It's acid peat land, all gorse, bracken and bilberries. It looked surprisingly like the landscape I'd just left. The ancient woodlands had been recently managed to allow light in. The under-storey had largely been ripped out and had a torn, battered look. Unlike us, Nature has no issue with change, and by spring it would look different again as she clothed the ground in ephemerals until more trees leafed out into new space. But now the woodland floor looked horrific, huge tractor tyre marks making ditches in the soft, unburdened soil, the smell of fresh timber chipped and ripped, and the red-and-white tape cordoning off the whole area as if it was some crime scene. Ming found a large and beautiful piece of oak, naturally curved into a bowl shape, and we poked about, looking at the remaining trees, twisted into odd shapes from years of tight growing.

Ming and Sarah had mapped their park much as they had mapped the streets of Birmingham, this time through mushrooms: good ceps here, fly agarics over there, strange slime moulds and ink caps. Where they didn't map mushrooms, they saved wildlife. Ming and the dogs had found a ferret that she bravely – catching one is not easy – coaxed out with dog treats and bundled up in her coat. It lived with her and Sarah for a while before they found a ferret refuge. There was also a young green woodpecker they rescued from a gang of marauding crows and safely returned to its wood, and a young crow that didn't make it despite their love. Perhaps I was another wild thing needing rescuing.

I stayed long enough to be able to contemplate driving again and left their kind, warm hospitality to go somewhere that was actually home. I returned to my parents, three days before Christmas, without a present to my name and eyes raw from crying. I felt the defeat that comes with crawling home, but I also knew that, however wounded my pride, I had a home to crawl to. As the landscape changed from acid to chalk and the motorway banks dazzled with the silvery seed heads of old man's beard, each seed with its own streamer to keep it afloat in the air so it can find new territory, I was glad I knew where I was heading.

I felt safe on the chalk and flint. I knew what to expect of it, how it would smear in the rain, how it would smell after frost. I drove into the setting sun blinded by the golden wet road. I drove to a place that, finally, I didn't need a map for.

30

I found out from my parents that H had gone back into hospital. He'd spend Christmas there and into New Year, as he fought off an infection. This was bleak news. He'd move out in January. I was overwhelmed by the thought of him alone, but I could do nothing to help: he didn't want me to visit and slowly I stopped asking. I was in a liminal space, both physically and metaphorically, so I took to walking again.

I walked to Denbury Hill fort on a bleak day, the grey of the sky flooding the landscape. I stomped around with the dog on the ramparts, looking for something, anything. I peered at the seed heads of old man's beard and clumps of eupatorium, looking for answers, but there were none to be found.

I walked to the back of the fort where great beeches and yews lined its banks. The banks were sodden and slippery, smeared by feet that had been running up and down. I wondered why anyone would choose to do that on such a steep bank, and when I lifted my gaze from the grey soil I saw a swing, made from a branch and thick, blue nylon rope. It, too, was occupying a liminal space, hanging just out of reach of the bank, twelve feet or so. I launched myself at it and, with great effort, managed to clamber onto the seat and sit hanging. I saw I could get back to the ground unscathed only with momentum and started to swing my legs. Each time I missed the top of the bank, but I was unwilling to jump off and land in the mud. The dog looked on, unimpressed, and I sat, swinging gently, trying to figure out my next move.

After a while my swing began to arch and I realised why the bank was a mud slide. The swing's architect had made a good decision: it was a perfect arch, reaching high into the tree tops and back to the bank. I started to gain momentum and lean back into the swing, swirling around the dark-grey branches of the beeches against a leaden sky. I went back and forth, back and forth. The dog wandered off to explore and I let go of something. Not enough to change anything, but enough to forget for a few seconds. I gained courage, and when I next passed over the bank, I leapt. It was not a graceful exit but I arrived on land in one piece, if a little muddy, and went to find the dog, who was waiting by another swing.

This one had a much longer rope and was low to the ground, tied to a long, arching branch. The floor there was all beech leaves, seeping out the last of their copper hue. If the last swing required moxy to jump onto it, this required no more than that I face the tree, push myself on against its trunk and lie back.

It had a long, low, graceful arch that gained quickly. Soon I was both high and fast on it. I looked up at the sky and the many tips of the beech trees reaching up, as I swirled and swung, mesmerised by that unexpected playground. I thought of all the lovely boughs I had seen over the canals and wished for rope swings there. I thought of the unknown swing-makers of my childhood. There was a wonderful highly dangerous swing by a bridge that, at the peak of its arch, took you over the railway. My mother always warned me never to use it, and I never did, though I often went to look at it. There were swings that went over rivers and ponds, and swings that took in grassy mounds and left you with nothing but blue sky.

After a good hour of swinging I was ready to place my feet firmly on the ground. The dog and I walked around the remaining ramparts and down the hill to the car, sliding through puddles. We returned home mud-splattered and tired, but the minute I was around people again, my panic was back. I worried about my future, about H's future, about Charlotte's future. I returned to my broken record, adding more grooves to my worries.

My father handed me T. H. White's *England Has My Bones*, and for several hours I put aside my worries. 'Falling in love is a desolating experience, but not when it is with the countryside,' wrote White. The next day I walked around muddy fields flecked with flint. I found an old bridle path that passed an ancient woodland. Clematis and ivy had tied the hedgerow trees together so that they made one long tunnel. At various points there were flint cobbles and at others a deep slick of mud to skid through. Dog's mercury lined the under-storey, and every now and then there was a great majestic oak, its limbs like lightning against the low light of the morning. I walked the bridle path in a dream, drenched every now and again by fierce sunbeams. Eventually I hit a road and wandered home. I did that walk repeatedly for the next week though it was never as charming as it was on the first day. It seemed to get muddier and I sweated more each time.

Eventually my mother put a stop to all that wandering. I had been away from my house for almost a month, wandering, driving, wandering, and the fear of returning had started to eat at me. I sat down with my mother and sister and told them that all I really wanted to do was return to my home, clear up the mess and leave, so that when I really had to go back, I knew what was waiting. Without missing a beat, my mother suggested we go immediately.

Four hours later, after several painfully slow traffic jams, we opened the front door to be confronted by boxes and packing peanuts. H had ordered a box of packing peanuts so large that it couldn't get through the door. Instead he'd distributed small boxes of them everywhere. It was clear the exhaustion of packing had worn him thin. The house looked as if someone had just sat down and said, 'No more.'

Alone, I wouldn't have been able to face it, but my mother was practical. Her no-nonsense attitude soon had it back into order. She scrubbed, polished, tidied and threw out a great number of things, while I seemed mostly to rearrange books. By the next day, it was a house full of boxes still, but there was space to breathe. She walked around saying, 'This is a lovely house.' I saw it through her eyes. It was a lovely house, I thought. It was my house, lovingly made for a marriage that was no more.

I'd often thought how much I wished H had said he wanted to keep it, how a new beginning would have been much easier for me, but I understood now what a gift he'd left me with. We had poured so much love into the space and it could be mine again, if I could remain kind to it, to him, to me.

I longed for Charlotte to see my home, my belongings, my books, trinkets and photos. She longed for this too. We knew that the empty space in our relationship was becoming impossible. I often felt like a person of many rucksacks, always leaving. I'd become so used to carrying everything with me that when I did come home I was startled by how many possessions I had. I'd felt sometimes that I could reject all of those things, but at others I'd longed for my favourite teacup or to water some houseplants.

My mother's favourable view reminded me that I did belong somewhere: I had a home, and it came with a past I could not reject. We left the following day and I closed the door to an ordered, calmer space.

On the way back my mother said, 'You've been walking in hope of finding solitude, but it doesn't work like that. If you walk in a rage you walk the rage with you. Solitude, I think, for you and me, comes only with being content and that, I think, comes with being still. You need to get back into gardening. You don't need to rage across the countryside any more. You need to slow down.'

I thought about my messy garden with that happy blackbird still merrily harvesting grapes rotting on the vine and singing about it. The garden would take a number of months to get back into something other than wild. I didn't want any grand plans or to impose order to tackle it. After a year of mostly leaving it be, I'd found new secrets in its space, but I wanted to be part of it again. I wanted to be part of its rhythm, to expand with the lengthening days, to grow with it and harvest what was mine at the end. Now that I knew how much the blackbirds loved my grapes, I'd always leave some for them, but next year I didn't want to watch all the fruit rot back into the ground. I wanted to taste the garden again.

Before I left I found a half-empty packet of 'Winter Density' lettuce under a pile of books and emptied it onto several pots with the skeletons of tomatoes. It was an almost absent-minded gesture – why throw seeds into the bin when they can disappear into the soil? When I returned again, every little seed had a root bent out of it, wiggling into the soil below. It was a mild winter and it shouldn't have surprised me that the lettuce germinated, but it did. I checked daily on the seeds, remarking at their progress, too thickly scattered seeds that mostly wouldn't amount to much. The weather would turn, but life had sprung forth in a few pots by the back door and that was enough. There was my mother's contentment in a few pale seeds on some spent compost.

* * *

I was beginning to understand why I had howled in the Hebrides with the wind. I was grieving. It was not so much a recovery process because I think you can recover from leaving a marriage, but I'm not sure you can recover from leaving the responsibility of caring. Or perhaps in years to come I will learn that you can recover, but that it is a long journey. Instead I think my grief was around the end of a story. I had always imagined that I would be there till the very end. Now I might be there at the very end, but more likely I might not. I will not be there in the same way. H had said that to me months ago, and I was furious, but he was right. Nobody knows when that ending is coming or what it might look like, but I thought I would be there. Living with cystic fibrosis had been difficult, heartbreaking, tormenting, but also all the other, diametrically opposite things to that. Joyous, loving and fulfilling. Now my road led elsewhere. Thus I was grieving an ending, a marriage and a house, and I was also celebrating a beginning, and a love that was unlike anything before it.

Part of my grief then was also this. I had found someone I didn't want at any cost to let go. But you have to, of course. You cannot hold onto the things you most want because everything is lost eventually. Everything stops, everything ends, your heart, my heart, the rain, the wind, even the sun. So to find yourself letting go of one thing to hold onto another is complicated. Part of my grief lay in how complicated it felt to admit that this new love, if taken from me, might leave a hole that was impossible to fill. I had built loss into my life. I'd thought I was well versed in future loss, but now the landscape looked entirely different.

31

I decided to spend New Year's Day in Birmingham and drove back on New Year's Eve. Dave and Louise invited me to spend the evening at the basin. Seeing in the New Year on the water seemed fitting and I accepted. H welcomed in the New Year in hospital, the infection subsiding slowly, but it was clear that it had left him very weak. By the end of the month he was supposed to have moved into his new home. Was I a monster for wanting this to happen? Who moves a sick man on? I looked at his packed stuff, the boxes carefully labelled with contents and rooms, such as 'Fragile bisque ware, back bedroom'. Were these the statements of a man ready to go?

I needed to own that threshold, to pass from one year into the next as quietly as I could. At ten o'clock on New Year's Eve, I packed the boat in a rucksack with an eight-pack of beer, some bike lights, waterproofs, a high-visibility jacket and a lifejacket. Then I took the number thirty-five bus into town and wove slowly through the city, trying to decide the best place to get into the water. In the end, after a long and rather hot walk, I got in at Five Ways on the Birmingham and Worcester Branch. I was a little nervous of the towpath at night, so I blew up the boat above ground and skipped down, launching myself into the water in one swift move so that I didn't attract any unwanted attention. Once I was on the water I turned on all the bike lights and put on the high-visibility jacket.

The water was still, inky black and so calm that it was like paddling through the finest silk. The sides of the towpath loomed up, dark shadows every now and then illuminated by the soft neon glow of a streetlight or a sitting-room window. I was warm from walking and didn't need gloves. I saw my first few towpath users, young women seemingly drunk but perhaps just teetering on precarious heels. I passed a moored narrowboat and the owner, catching sight of the bike lights, peered out through a window and waved me on.

I went through a bridge hole, which was a little terrifying as it narrowed – if anyone was under the bridge I'd be an easy target. I turned off the lights and floated silently through. It was empty, and I continued on into the blackness. There was a steep bank of ivy that fluttered in a breeze, my bike lights catching the sheen of the leaves. I'd thought I might see a lot of rats, but the water was smooth, a flawless black mirror.

As I turned up Holliday Passage, I saw a goose floating in the middle of the water, asleep, its head tucked under a wing. What a strange place to sleep with the bright lights of the Mailbox and all the noisy passers-by – within metres, the canal had gone from eerily silent to bustling, as bars lined the sides and the heavy boom of bad R&B blared out of old wharf buildings. I decided not to disturb the goose and warily paddled to the left of it. It spun around and floated towards me. I saw that the neck was not tucked under a wing, but snapped back, the chin facing upwards, the legs still extended for paddling. Another dead thing on the canal. I wondered if Ming would want to stuff it, but I wasn't sure that dragging a dead goose into the next year would be auspicious, so I stared at it for a while, wondering how it had broken its neck. It floated away as the breeze rippled the water.

I thought of the duck mussels as I floated over them, and all the bream, carp, tench, rudd, roach and ruffe that floated between the eels and the pike. I thought of water insects, the nymphs and larvae, fish eggs and things even smaller. Of them floating and swimming in the dark waters while the bright lights of the city mirrored back life.

As the towpath life busied, I got many invitations to take travellers along with me. I politely declined. I met several police officers, who greeted me merrily. A young girl handed her coat to her mate and posed against the tunnel in the tiniest of tops on the highest of heels. I passed under the basin bridge and called Dave on my phone to tell him I'd arrived.

I passed into a dark patch and out again into the glow of an old streetlamp that illuminated a brick passage onto the street. It felt very Dickensian, the warm glow of light, the brick patina against the lime mortar, the light pooling on the towpath and the water.

Paddling at night was delightful. I felt safe in the middle of the water, able to go leisurely and take in detail. No one expected me to be there and I liked the quiet, passing through.

I turned right after the bridge into the basin, and the huge prows of the oldest boats loomed out at me. They were magnificent at night. Tarred black, with glossy painted rims, those old working boats sit much higher on the water than modern narrowboats. I floated up and touched one gently, that great beast sitting there. Then I heard Dave open the front of his boat. He and our friend Saima appeared against a backdrop of stars. I handed over the beer and my waterproofs, and promised to be back before midnight.

I carried on under Broad Street Tunnel and up towards the ICC, waving to the merry, the drunk and the downright lost. A few more police officers wished me a good night and I let the boat drift into neon reflections, rippling from bars and streetlights, lying back in the quiet of the water while above ground the world partied on.

Suddenly I felt cold. My legs were wet from the run-off of paddling, my fingers a little numb, and midnight was fast approaching. I had thought about staying out on the water, but the warmth of Dave's cabin, the wood burner, the thought of beer and something to eat seemed far more appealing. I turned and paddled back fast to gain some heat. The gangway to Dave's boat was at least five foot above mine so I meandered around, looking for a suitable place to haul myself out. The gates to the basin were firmly locked so I'd have to squeeze between narrowboats and pull myself up onto the Worcester Bar. I dipped under a chain and floated up to the end of one boat, moored horizontally to the Bar, and pulled myself out, then the boat. I carried it onto Dave's and rapped at the metal door.

As I pulled back the top hatch the warmth flooded out and I could smell food. I dropped down into the cabin and was quickly issued with beer. Dave was dancing at one end, Louise offered a variety of dishes and Saima swayed gently. I felt decidedly sober as I sank a beer, ate cheese and sweet things, and told them of my paddling adventure.

At midnight we crawled out of the warmth to stand on the Worcester Bar, drink harsh whisky and watch the fireworks. It was a great place, quiet and dark, yet surrounded by the bright lights of the city. A penthouse apartment let off its own firework display, if somewhat slow and disjointed. We heard countdowns and horns blaring, wished each other a prosperous new year and drank more of the whisky a developer had sent to sweeten the boaters for some monstrosity they wanted to park on a tiny patch of land the boats moored against. For the first time in recent memory the basin was to have its first baby and there was genuine joy that someone might grow up among the residents. I called Charlotte to wish her happiness and heard the tail end of the London fireworks.

We went back indoors and ate more, but it was time for me to leave. I rolled up the boat and left it at Dave's, unsure how to get home. With luck I flagged a passing taxi and was home by two a.m.

I found the dog curled up in my unpacked rucksack by the door as if to say, 'God knows where you're heading next, but

I know you won't leave without this.' I felt a pang of guilt, but it looked a snug, sensible place to sleep if you weren't feeling quite sure of things. We went to bed, lulled to sleep by the owls hooting.

32

I have a little tradition on New Year's Day. I like to spend it doing something I want to do a lot more of. Walking somewhere unknown, doing something new or old, reading a book, cooking a new dish, that sort of thing. I was fuzzy-headed and tired, but I'd agreed with my neighbour to go to the allotment, which was something I now ached to do more of. This coming year, I wouldn't take myself away from the thing I loved dearly. This year I would garden again.

Along with neglecting my soil, my garden and my seeds, I had neglected to fix my shed roof and now everything was damp and had an impressive blue dusting of mould. I found some corrugated-iron sheets and laid them over the roof, weighing them down with planks. A fix that would last as long as the first gust of wind. I moved my bee-keeping equipment to the dry side of the shed and composted the unharvested asparagus, and the sodden kale seed heads.

I rooted around in the mess and found a fork. The soil was kind, soft and pliable, ready to be worked gently. I removed all the herb bennet that was taking over the front of the allotment. Then, when I had the last of it out, I moved around the allotment, looking for dock and green alkanet, delighting in loosening the soil around deep taproots and gently plucking them out, as you might a satisfying splinter. Fleshy rooted alkanet and tenacious dock pulled from the sucking earth right to their very tips. Once

I had finished with that lot, I dumped them into a water butt to rot down into something else. I tackled the nettles with their spaghetti-yellow elastic roots, running carefully under them to loosen the soil so that I could trace their progress across bare ground as I uprooted them, handling them by the root, so the green parts swung upside down.

Next I went after the dandelions that had adopted the paths as their homes. Dandelion roots, much like dock, can go deep through hard compaction to find nutrients locked away from other green things. For this reason they can grow well in poor, hard soil. You can endlessly slice of their heads and they will endlessly laugh at your mistake. You have to remove around fifteen centimetres or so of tap root before they rot off. I like dandelions. I think they're very beautiful in flower and in seed. The unopened dandelion flower, when in bud, deep in the centre of the rosette with a little centimetre of root, a dandelion heart, if you like, gently fried in olive oil is as good as an artichoke, nutty, bitter, utterly delicious. But the kind of dandelions that grow in my paths don't offer up fleshy hearts. The leaves are thin and tough, no good for salads, and the roots fork too many times to peel and roast them. I levered them out of their homes and threw them into the weed soup to rot down.

A year of letting every foxglove seed meant I had a small army of them marching here and there. I carefully uprooted them and moved them to the back of the allotment where I have a puddle for a pond next to a dead hedge of rotting twigs. It is a thing of much life, the strange pothole of water, as is its rotting neighbour, full of beetle haunts and secret caves where many things hide, slime moulds creep and mushrooms burst forth. I love my dead hedge. I have spent many an afternoon peering into its recesses, imagining myself small enough to explore that strange horizontal woodland, but it is not a thing of beauty. It is a pile of rotting twigs and tough stems. The foxgloves were my attempt at decorating it. I took the many rosettes that had merrily sown themselves across my good soil and carefully tucked them into errant holes. I've found that the foxgloves, if moved when the world is damp and mild, will happily bed themselves back in and flower majestically come summer. I awarded the dead hedge a fringe of rosettes and stood back to admire it. I pulled a few leaves out of the puddle and topped it up with rainwater.

When I'd finished decorating I wandered down with the dog to the giant mountain of rotting chippings the local tree surgeon had left us and hunted through the various piles, cracking open the mountains, mining for what was on its way to being compost. I filled barrow after barrow, heaving it back up the hill where the bonfire moss waits patiently each autumn to rejuvenate in the tired concrete path cracks and turn the slope of the hill a brilliant green. I pushed past where the best black-berries grow, past where the rats, cats and foxes have bent the bottom of the fence so they can run freely when we're not around, past where the honesty weaves itself into the fence to bring some joy, past where the philadelphus hangs over from the park, past where the ivy and holly make such a dense barrier along the fence. I spread thick layers of rotting chip-pings to suppress the weeds and keep the soil warm over winter. I did this till I was exhausted and someone suggested we cele-brate the New Year with a pint at the pub. I had mud under my nails, twigs in my hair. I had soil on my knees, my fingers ached from pulling things up and I was very happy. I was con-tent. I felt quiet inside.

I looked at the pile of weeds, many of which I had been following along the edges of canals. There I had celebrated their ordinariness; I had championed their tenacity to survive and grow; I had admired them for being something other than a weed.

I had spent a summer watching them grow, watching them take over my garden and gain ground on my allotment, watching their reflections in canal water, watching pollinators land happily on them, watching them survive or not in our wasteland. And now I was pulling them out again. It's a funny game, gardening. For, let's face it, there is very little in the act that benefits the garden. It is nearly all for the gardener: deciding what should stay and go is an act of arrogance.

We make some fine-looking spaces. We pull off some extraordinary flourishes of flowering, picking plants from around the world. We eat well from the act. But when I think back to some of the canal edges or railway banks, the wild birch woodland that grows out of the glass factory ruins at the beginning of Icknield Loop, the buddleja that have rejoiced with butterflies out of the crumbling brick wall by the Engine Arm Aqueduct, those flowering rushes and irises that danced in the pool of a disused boat hull, the mushrooms that sprouted between crisps packets, the moss-scapes that covered ugly concrete, and the liverworts that have hidden our hardscaping sins, it is hard to think of even my best achievement in gardening as good.

33

Endings are never quite as you expect. My marriage did not end on a metal walkway in west London when I first saw Charlotte. It did not end because I fell in or out of love. It ended when I decided to survive. It was not about choosing happiness: coming out has many joys to it, but there is sadness too, the loss of time, grappling with a sense of dishonesty to yourself, to others. It came down to one simple thing in the end: stay put, stay silent and crack, or take the first move and get to where you should be going.

We change, our world changes. In part, isn't that why we like to move, to travel? To see change at a pace we choose. And isn't that in part why we hate change we feel we had no say in? The selling-off of green space, the gentrification that crams in housing with no greenery or play space? The canals I learnt to love will not stay the same. They have changed a lot since their beginning, but they have also changed very little: everything is subtle and ordinary.

Many of our canals were abandoned, a change that is rarely mentioned. Between the Second World War and the late 1960s, huge swathes of the network across the UK were either turned into drainage ditches full of detritus or became unnavigable through lack of maintenance. Some were sold off privately. There was little or no tourist trade and you weren't allowed to navigate on Saturdays and Sundays. The canals were undervalued and under-derused, a neglected resource.

In 1930, Tom Rolt, conqueror of canals, prose poet and engineer, bought a horse-drawn boat called *Cressy* and later wrote *Narrow Boat*, a tale of navigating a now lost world of canals and boats after the war. Consider it a *Cider with Rosie* for the waterways. In 1946, he and the literary agent Robert Aickman created the Inland Waterways Association to campaign for greater use of canals. The association attracted interest: Peter Scott, of the Wetlands Trust, was an early member, becoming its vice president, as was the author Elizabeth Jane Howard, who was its secretary until her first novel was published.

While the arterial roads were built for a new fast and furious post-war Britain, the canals withdrew into the shadows, a physical shadow without water to reflect back life. What should have been a ribbon of still water winding its way from our cities to rural towns and out into meadows and fields was no more. Some canals burst their banks and locks failed. Other waterways became choked with weeds and fallen trees, silted up, and started to become land once more, rather than a water body. Many bits of canal were seen as redundant and filled in, built on, a lost footprint under shopping malls and housing developments. They vanished off maps and, as they were not a natural watercourse, who would argue? A dedicated gang of volunteers dug out, cleared up and rebuilt numerous stretches. *Narrow Boat* was an unexpected hit, and a new generation of enthusiasts, leisure boaters, began to fill the canals with life.

* * *

Travelling on the canals is to carry out a series of small rituals, to bear witness to the way the light changes on the surface of the water or a seed head disperses and where next year's plants appear. The best journeys are always worth repeating, and that is how I feel about my favourite stretches of the canals. I like those cathedrals of green trees in the suburbs. I like them in spring when the fresh new green unfurls. I loved them in autumn when those buttery leaves swirled around my paddle, and now in the stark of winter when I see their bare bones swaying in the wind as I feel the chill of the water beneath me.

I see now that this journey on the water was about finding an external correlation to my inner world. I needed a transmutable world, a fluid space that would allow me to make my own changes.

The canals will change again and again. Those metal hulls will sink or be dragged out, the edges tidied, the graffiti removed. I hope there will always be kingfishers and butterflies to watch; I hope later generations will watch herons spear fish and lean over the edge of their boats to peer at pike. I hope that everyone has the sense to leave a little of the edges wild. I hope that that dad and his son get a boat and that I meet them on the water one day. Nature will always find her spot, eke out her living in the most uncompromising places. There will always be wayside weed.

* * *

I was running towards rather than away, and the canals were my journey to where I am. We tell stories and draw maps to make sense of who we are, where we are, why we are. Sometimes we get stuck telling the wrong story about ourselves: the story does the telling, when it should be the other way round. Some stories come to abrupt endings or fall apart and you try to finish them off or start a new chapter and you can't: they've ended. Places tell stories. Geography is a story, and so is ecology. We make sense of our whole world, the immediate, intimate and the wider one, through stories. We are a species that is bound by, wrapped up in and perhaps only functions because of stories. Perhaps it is why we are moved when we hear that elephants have burial grounds and mourning spots; other species tell stories too. My garden tells a story: every day it gets up and sings its tale, inviting others to play their part. I remember that whenever I hear the buzz of a bee or the haunting hoot of the owls at night. That story then becomes part of my story. The players, the land are ways by which I navigate, a compass to find home again.

* * *

I have a map pinned to my wall that traces a strange summer, a turbulent autumn and, at times, a desolate winter. I can run my finger down lines that trace a map of friendship. On certain stretches of the map, all I can see is friendship: I hear Sarah laughing; I taste the bitter hops of a shared beer with Ming; I smell the water and the engine oil of Dave's boat. I hear Clare's voice on the phone. I feel the glow of Charlotte's love.

My map is peopled. That is how I got here, dragged along, sometimes physically, by people like when Ming and Sarah tied my boat to theirs and rowed me to the end. Pulled, pushed and jollied along by those I love. And now I'm here I'm a little more me, a little less too. I only got here because of people. I can admit that now. I'd like to write a long list of all those who got me here. It'd make a great map.

My map is peopled but it's also planted. For those wayside weeds, those dainty and those not so, that willowed and wisped in the wind, they got me here too. They offered a reprieve from all the opinions and voices. I was, as we all are, unjudged by weeds and rats. There's something poetic about that. 'You don't like me and I don't care,' say the feral things that creep and grow in our filth. Or 'You may like me here but wouldn't want me somewhere more refined.' We are outsiders together, I have thought. We are outsiders and survivors. That's the point about unsettled ecology, the feral and the weedy: they understand the comedy of survival. Do it at all costs or end in tragedy.

I understand that now. I think H always got it.

By the end of the month he had moved out to start a new life in a new house. I was to do the same thing in an old house. I moved furniture, repainted, filled the rooms with houseplants, added an armchair and ordered my library so I could read in the afternoon sun, dappled by the tropical foliage of my plants. I gardened my interior. Then I went outside and did the same. After a bit Charlotte came and gardened with me and I went home with her and did the same. We're very good at gardening together. It may be what we do best.

I don't need the watery world of the canals to represent anything now, other than a wonderful bit of nature, a ribbon of green space like no other. The boat and I, we're sticking together for I, over all those days on the water, have learnt this much. I love a woman and I love my boat, and I hope that both these things continue far into my future, to the point that I can trace on the map and off it.

Acknowledgements

Hidden at the end of sentences, between paragraphs and at the end of chapters Lucy Reid and Richard Hawley have kept me together. They may not be visible in this book, but their presence is very much felt. I count a great deal of my happiness to you and your lovely family.

There are many heartfelt thanks to be said, in particular to Ming and Sarah for the adventures that have been and all that are around the corner. Your love and friendship means the world to me. To Dave Paine for boats, beer and botanising. To Holiday for respecting me as a writer.

To Clare Savage for listening and listening and listening. You are the best of bests.

To Sue and Les, Ingrid and Jeremy, Saima Razzaq, Jane Perone, Anne from the allotment, Birgit and Nick, Juliet and Louise, Andrew and Siobhan, Fionnula Ardee, Ella McSweeney, Fab and Vicki, Jamie Bradley, Juliet C, Lorna, Louise, Pip McKnight, Lisa and Rachel, William 'Billy' Foreman, Cynthia, Alex Zafiris, Mark D (for writing the best letter anyone could receive on coming out), Adrian (for giving me the idea for the book in the first place) and Ian Francis for those obscure and brilliant canal songs.

To The Canal and River Trust and for the countless volunteers who keeping the waters flowing.

To Rupert Lancaster for such steady, kind, unwavering support and to all those at Hodder and Stoughton who've helped me to here. Thanks to Hazel Orme for her careful and thoughtful editing throughout.

To Charlotte for sticking by and holding on, for leaping and soaring, for following and leading, for looking outward and in, for always holding my hand.

To Virginia Rankin for being there and here, on the page, for me.

To my family, Becca and Jonny for listening way beyond sibling duty. My Dad for filling me with words and to my Mum for letting them all out.

Text Acknowledgements

Extract from 'Born Yesterday' from THE LESS DECEIVED by Philip Larkin. Reprinted with the permission of Faber & Faber Ltd.

Excerpt from Richard Brautigan's 'Blackberry Motorist' from REVENGE OF THE LAWN. Copyright © 1971 by Richard Brautigan; Renewal Copyright © 1999, by Ianthe Brautigan Swenson. Reprinted with the permission of the Estate of Richard Brautigan; all rights reserved.

An invitation from the publisher

Join us at www.hodder.co.uk, or follow us
on Twitter @hodderbooks to be a part of
our community of people who love the very
best in books and reading.

Whether you want to discover more about a book
or an author, watch trailers and interviews, have the
chance to win early limited editions, or simply browse
our expert readers' selection of the very best books,
we think you'll find what you're looking for.

And if you don't, that's the place to tell us what's missing.

We love what we do, and we'd love you to be a part of it.

www.hodder.co.uk

 @hodderbooks

HodderBooks

HodderBooks